BELLYDANCE

Books LLC®, Wiki Series, Memphis, USA, 2011. ISBN: 9781156404188. www.booksllc.net
Copyright: http://creativecommons.org/licenses/by-sa/3.0/deed.en

Table of Contents

Belly dancers
Amar Gamal 1
Amelia Zidane 2
Amera Eid 2
Ariellah Aflalo 3
Didem (belly dancer) 4
Dina Talaat 7
Estelle Asmodelle 7
Fifi Abdou 8
Ghawazi 9
Maria Jammal 10
Nadia Gamal 10
Nagwa Fouad 11
Naima Akef 11
Nejla Ates 12
Nelly Mazloum 12
Rachel Brice 14
Rozeta Ahalyea 15
Samia Gamal 15
Serena Wilson 16
Shakira 17
Taheyya Kariokka 26
Terezka Drnzik 27
Zeinat Olwi 28

Bellydance
American Bellydancer 28
American Tribal Style Belly Dance .. 28
Belly dance 29
Bellydance Superstars 34
Gothic bellydance 35
Hoochie coochie 35
Improv Tribal Style Belly Dance 36
Köçek 38
Raqs sharqi 39
Sandstorm: The Jim Boz Dance Company 40
Talisman Dance Company 40
The Indigo Belly Dance Company 41
Tribal Fusion (dance form) 41
Çiftetelli 42
Čoček 43

Introduction

Purchase of this book entitles you to a free trial membership in the publisher's book club at www.booksllc.net. (Time limited offer.) Simply enter the barcode number from the back cover onto the membership form. The book club entitles you to select from hundreds of thousands of books at no additional charge. You can also download a digital copy of this and related books to read on the go. Simply enter the title or subject onto the search form to find them.

Each chapter in this book ends with a URL to a hyperlinked online version. Type the URL exactly as it appears. If you change the URL's capitalization it won't work. Use the online version to access related pages, websites, footnotes, tables, color photos, updates. Click the version history tab to see the chapter's contributors. Click the edit link to suggest changes.

A large and diverse editor base collaboratively wrote the book, not a single author. After a long process of discussion and debate, the chapters gradually took on a neutral point of view reached through consensus. Additional editors expanded and contributed to chapters striving to achieve balance and comprehensive coverage. This reduced the regional or cultural bias found in many other books and provided access and breadth on subject matter otherwise little documented.

Amar Gamal

Amar Gamal (born c. 1975) is a well known Cuban dancer who practices the art of bellydancing. She lived in Florida as a teenager.

At the age of thirteen, Gamal began performing as a bellydancer with the Mid-Eastern Dance Exchange company, based in Miami Beach. One of her directors at the time was the well-known dancer, Tamalyn Dallal.

Gamal went on to become the first dancer to audition with bellydancing techniques and be accepted at the New World School of the Arts' Performing Arts School. She trained in other types of dancing, such as ballet, jazz, tap, flamenco and modern, while at that school. Gamal subsequently went on to dance for five different dance companies.

Gamal graduated with a degree in psychology at Bridgewater State College in Massachusetts. Her career expanded after that, as Gamal was given an opportunity to perform during the NFL's Super Bowl XXIX in 1995, and she earned the Miss World of Belly-dancing contest in 1996.

In 1997, Gamal had the opportunity of performing during the Gianni Versace fashion show. In 1998, she participated at the Oriental Dance Production, in Lexington, Kentucky.

Gamal's celebrity kept growing during the late 1990s, and she toured many places around the world. She has performed in countries like Trinidad & Tobago, Haiti and Costa Rica.

2002 proved to be a pivotal year for Gamal's career: She earned the Mondo

Melodia Bellydance Breakbeats first place award on May 14 and was chosen to participate in the release tour of a CD — *Bellydance Superstars* — released on November 12.

Gamar is also a bellydancing teacher and has taught in Los Angeles and San Francisco, California, in New York city and in Buenos Aires, Argentina.
Source (edited): "http://en.wikipedia.org/wiki/Amar_Gamal"

Amelia Zidane

Amelia Zidane . born in Grenoble (France), from Algerian parents, was attracted very early by the music, the dance and the theater despite her family's reticence. She studied socio-medical sciences intending herself to become children's psychologist but her artistic passion, drove her to leave her province to Paris in 1994 to pursue her dream. She worked several jobs before being noticed by Jacques Boni, Director of the **"Trois Mailletz"** in Paris, where she will move forward from 1997 to 2005.

She choreographs and directs her own spectacles, creating about fifteen shows of one hour and half each, true Showgirl, she creates in 1995 **Flamenco-Arabic** then in the 2001 **"Oriental-Modern-Dance-Show"**, a fusion between hip hop and belly dance. She danced in the biggest world theatres, such as Bercy with Khaled, the Zenith with Cheb Mami, Olympia with Enrico Macias, Manu Chao in Toulouse and Central Park in New York … Two European tours and a world tour are followed from there, we estimate at more than 600.000 spectators having applauded in it.

In 1999, Amelia Zidane records **"Sefina"** a title which she Co-written and interpreted in Arabic, produced by EMC Records, after a pasage noticed on Hit Machine she settles in Beirut where she presents "Paris-Beirut". She collaborates with the famous **D.J Said Mrad** and **Adam Youssef** on the recording of an album.

"l'Orientale Fatale" will make you travel through the Magical World of Arabian Night… Amelia Zidane is one of the most renowned belly dancer in the world.

Amelia Zidane was the 1st belly dancer to appear on the Covers of French Magazines, *Elle*, *TéléMag* …

"She leans as a queen and goes back like a dream. Whoever saw her on the stage did not regret his coming & whoever missed her will catch her when she gets back and would confirm that Amelia Zidane lightens up literally the screen." Aziz Patel.

Pioneer and innovative, in 2007, Amelia Zidane imagined, created and developed with i-magic: The First World Belly Dance Championship **"Hezzi ya nawaem"**

Her contribution added to the success of the TV show broadcasted on **LBCI** at prime time (watched in the Middle East and around the world), where her personal input as a consultant, coach and member of the jury with **Simon Asmar**, **Najwa Fouad**, **Zaza Hassan**, **Nadra Assaf** were an added value. An experience renewed in 2008 with **"Hezzi ya nawaem 2"** as a casting director and consultant.

2008-2009 Amelia is choreographer, dancer and member of jury on **"Ajwaa"** at prime time on **Futur TV**

New Year's Eve 2009, Amelia Zidane was on Prime Time on **LBC** with **Tony Baroud**, **Melhem Barakat**, **Yara**. June 2010 **J&B** sponsorised Amelia at the **Global Party Byblos** / August: Nahide & Al Jamal Istanbul Turkey July 2010 Amelia Zidane Live at **BEITEDDINE PALACE** August 2010 Amelia performed with **TIESTO** in Egypt. Amelia is the Official Bellydancer of The **Prince Abdel-Aziz ben Fahd ben Abdel-Aziz al-Saoud**

Amelia Zidane Awarded **SEXIEST BELLY DANCER OF THE WORLD 2010** by Fanoos .
Source (edited): "http://en.wikipedia.org/wiki/Amelia_Zidane"

Amera Eid

Amera Eid is an Australian bellydancer and owner of an Australian bellydance school, Amera's Palace. Amera is of Egyptian and European background and was introduced to bellydancing at the age of twelve. She began her professional training with Rozeta Ahalyea in Sydney in 1983 and worked the Sydney restaurant and Arabic nightclub circuit. She appeared as a support act in concerts for numerous visiting Arabic singers such as Mona Merashli, George Wassouf, Rageb Alame, Rabih El Kholi, Amr Diab, Ehab Toufik, Melham Baraket, Tony Mohanna, Mayez Al Bayah, Pascal Mashalany, and Nawal El Zoughby.Template:Jerusalem Hotel Amman Jordan 1991

Eid opened Amera's Palace bellydance boutique in 1987, which included one of the first bellydance schools in Sydney. (The school operated in Sheiks Tent nightclub on weeknights , whilst the nightclub was closed in 1987) In the days before the internet the boutique also acted as the hub of information on bellydancing in Australia through The Palace newsletter, which ultimately became a bi annual magazine. The magazine merged with Bellydance Oasis Magazine in late 2006 due to Amera's growing commitments to looking after three foster children.

In 1990, Amera was put in contact with Lebanese agent Toros Siranossian, and became one of only a handful of non-Arabic dancers to work with him at that time. Mr Siranossian represented Amera for the next 7 years, with continuous year-round contracts throughout the Middle East, taking up residence in Beirut as her home base. Between 1994 and 1999 Amera also traveled regularly to Egypt, where she trained with top choreographers Raqia Hassan, Ibrahim Akef and Aida Nour, and also performed two contracts in the summer of 1999.

Amera returned to Australia after this and retired as a professional dancer but continuing to teach and runs international workshops . She is now also a fully qualified aerobics & fitness instructor. In 2008 she will be hosting THE FARHA TOUR to Australia, November 6-9th 2008, the first time a Belly Dance event of this international calibre has ever happened in the Southern Hemisphere.

Performances
- Amman Jordan Jerusalem hotel (2 months 1991, 1992 & 1993)
- Amman Jordan Intercontinental hotel (2 months 1994)
- Amman Jordan Regency Palace (2 months 1995)
- Aswan Basma Hotel (1999)
- Egypt Sharm el Sheik Gazala Gardens (1999)
- Greece Athens Shahraman Restaurant (4 months 1991)
- Greece Dubai Singapore New Caledonia (1985-1989)
- India New Delhi Hyatt Hotel (New Year's Eve 1989)
- Ivory Coast Abidjan - Al Sultan Restaurant (2 months 1995)
- Lebanon Beirut : Summerland Hotel (2 months New year 1995/96)
- Muscat Omman Al Bustan Palace (3 mths 1993)
- Syria Lattaquia Le Meridien (2 months 1994)
- Syria Le Meridien Hotel (2 months 1995)
- U.A.E Dubai Claridge hotel (2 months 1994 & 1996)
- U.A.E. Abu Dhabi Gulf Hotel (3 months 1992)
- U.A.E. Al Ain Intercontinental Hotel (2 months 1993 1994 & 1995)
- U.A.E. Al Ain Hilton Hotel (1 month 1992)
- U.A.E. Dubai St George hotel (2 months 1996)
- U.A.E. Dubai Carlton Tower hotel (2 months 1995)
- U.A.E. Dubai Vendome Plaza Hotel (2 months 1993 & 1994)

Source (edited): "http://en.wikipedia.org/wiki/Amera_Eid"

Ariellah Aflalo

Ariellah Aflalo is a contemporary Dark Fusion belly dancer, known for her dance technique and powerful stage presence. The signature dark flavor of her style, along with her skill as a dancer, has made her a legend in both the conventional and Gothic belly dance scenes.

Biography

Ariellah Aflalo grew up in California, raised in the traditions of her Moroccan heritage. She began to study classical ballet with the Royal Academy of Dance of London at the age of three and continued the training for the next 12 years. Upon moving to the San Francisco Bay Area, she took a hiatus from dance to complete her education and travel to Ivory Coast as a member of the Peace Corps.

After returning to the United States, Ariellah began studying folkloric North African belly dance under Janine Ryle. Janine was a student of Magana Baptiste and the renowned belly dance institution Hahbi 'Ru. Ariellah soon became a member of Janine's troupe, Dance Maghreb, which performed authentic Algerian and Berber dances. Seeing that the dance form was a natural fit for Ariellah, Janine encouraged her to seek instruction from the now-legendary Rachel Brice. Ariellah began studying Tribal Fusion belly dance with Rachel in 2002 and, a year later, became one of the founding members of Rachel's troupe, The Indigo Belly Dance Company.

When The Indigo began touring worldwide with the Bellydance Superstars, Ariellah chose to remain home where she could continue her personal dance projects and help nurture a fast-growing following of students. As the only stationary and locally accessible tie to The Indigo, as well as an innovator of Tribal Fusion belly dance in her own right, Ariellah quickly grew in popularity.

Photograph of Ariellah Aflalo. Image is under copyright of Pixie Vision Productions.
www.pixievisionproductions.com.

Goth scene influence

Ariellah was drawn into the goth scene in her teenage years. With an exotic background and appearance, she never quite fit in among her conventional peers but was embraced by the goth community. Ariellah began attending Death Guild — the longest-running goth club in San Francisco. There, the dance floor became an incubator for the personal style that she would later incorporate into belly dance. To this day, Ariellah continues to be involved in various artistic projects and events within the goth scene — locally, nationally, and across the world.

"Dark Fusion" belly dance

Ariellah's personal adaptation of Tribal Fusion belly dance gave birth to an offshoot style that she refers to as Dark Fusion. It preserves the fundamentals of traditional Middle Eastern belly dance technique, with a strict emphasis on posture and muscle isolations of the hips, stomach, shoulders, and chest. Unique to the style is a distinctive expression of dark emotion, frequently presented in theatrical fashion. The choice of music and costuming is often influenced by trends in the goth scene.

From Ariellah's website:
…in dark fusion belly dance performances, a deep emotion is invoked in the audience and there is a sense of the audience being brought into the performance. The energy that flows from the dancer is strong and piercing and draws the audience in with its expressiveness."
In 2007, Ariellah founded Deshret Dance Company (DDC). Under Ariellah's artistic direction, and with contributions from the troupe members, DDC became a vehicle for further exploration of Dark Fusion belly dance in the arena of group choreography and performance.

Projects

- Founding member of The Indigo Belly Dance Company
- Founder and artistic director of Deshret Dance Company
- Founding member of Noor Belly Dance Projeckt
- Original member of Danse Maghreb
- Co-founder and co-promoter of Shadow Dance
- Former co-promoter of Gothla US
- Performer and workshop instructor at numerous belly dance events across the world
- Guest performer at various goth clubs and underground events

Filmography

Instructional

- *Contemporary Belly Dance and Yoga Conditioning with Ariellah.* Produced by Neon and World Dance New York, World Dance New York.
- *Fantasy Belly Dance: Magic.* Produced by Neon and World Dance New York.

Performance

- *Gothic Belly Dance: The Darker Side of Fusion DVD.* Produced by Neon and World Dance New York, World Dance New York.
- *Gothic Belly Dance Volume II: Revelations.* Produced by Neon and World Dance New York, World Dance New York.
- *Bellydance Underworld.* Produced by Hollywood Music Center, Peko Records.
- *Tribal Revelations.* Produced by Neon and World Dance New York.

Source (edited): "http://en.wikipedia.org/wiki/Ariellah_Aflalo"

Didem (belly dancer)

Didem Kinali (born in 1986), known simply as **Didem**, is a Turkish Belly Dancer. She has been dancing since her childhood. She has gained some measure of international recognition since she started appearing on the live Turkish variety İbo Show, hosted by İbrahim Tatlıses. She is of Roma (Gypsy) ethnic heritage, a fact of which she is proud. Didem's mother is also a belly dancer and her father is a drummer.

Biography

Didem and her two siblings were raised in Kuştepe with her mother who immigrated from Saloniki, Greece, and her father from Yugoslavia. Although her mother was a belly dancer, Didem has said that her mother wasn't the one she learned from. Sema Yildiz, the famous Roma Turkish belly dancer, discovered Didem when she was a young teenager (13-14), and recognized her talent. Sema has also trained other famous Turkish belly dancers, including Asena, who was Ibrahim's belly dancer before Didem. Asena is also Sema's daughter.

Didem spent her first four years working at Sultana's Dinner and 1001 Nights Show in Istanbul, an institution close to Sema Yildiz and the belly dancing community, before entering the television domain on the İbo Show. She came in third in a contest held at this venue, but attracted a lot of attention nevertheless.

In August, 2008, İbrahim Tatlıses announced that Didem would no longer be dancing on his show, which she had been doing weekly for a couple of years. No reason was given, but as Didem, in her very first interview, mentioned going back to school (which she dropped out of at an early age to put all her energy into dancing), perhaps this is the reason. There have been a lot of rumours about her, as well as about Ibo. He talk-banned her when she started, because he wanted people to remember her by her dancing.

First interview with Didem

"I'm under protection courtesy of Mr. Tatlises"

Didem, known by many as the belly dancer of the *Ibo Show*, raised much curiosity due to the talk-ban issued on her by Ibrahim Tatlises. Widely known for her smile while dancing, contrary to the serious expression worn by many others, Didem decided to breach the talk-ban and answered many questions about her for *Yeni Aktuel* Magazine.

- I was born in 1986 in Gaziosmanpasa. Since I was raised in Kustepe, I'd rather say I'm from Kustepe (neighborhoods of Istanbul, t.n.) I have a brother and a sister. We are 'Romans' (oftentimes, 'Roman' people were attributed extraordinary talent in belly dancing and performing music for it, t.n.); mother immigrated from Saloniki, father from Yugoslavia. I spent all my childhood in Roman district, where we still live.

- I dropped out at my third year in primary school, then began dancing. I needed to work, but I loved dancing too much. Everywhere in our house are mirrors. Sometimes I dance for 24 hours on a stretch. When I feel like it, I turn the music on and begin dancing. Also, there's this Roman tradition; they put cymbals under a newborn daughter's pillow so she becomes a belly dancer when she grows up.
- I can't say I had a very happy childhood. I always wanted a bike but never had one due to financial reasons. I dropped out on my own decision, not my family's. I was a successful student except for maths. But I still want to study. I decided to complete my education. I'll even get a university degree.

Discovered in a contest

- Dancing talent runs in my family. My mother, Tulay, is a belly dancer as well. My father is the drummer Zeki Kinali. My grandfather is a retired oud (a kind of lute in Turkish Classical music) artist. My sister sings in weddings. My mother only taught me how to play cymbals. But I remember very well when my mother used to dance for extra pay; I used to hold onto her skirt. Then, I used to climb onto a table, dancing there while she danced on the stage. I was very enthusiastic about belly dancing. When my teacher asked me what would I be when I grew up, I always answered 'belly dancer'. But I couldn't dance this well if I weren't a Roman. I'm proud of being one.
- In wedding ceremonies, they called me to dance. Since my body is very flexible, my nickname was 'rubber-girl'. Now they call me 'Ibrahim's Belly-Dancer'
- I met Sema Yildiz, a belly-dance instructor. 'Let's find you a stage' she suggested. I was 13 or 14 years old then. I got transferred from the night clubs of Avcilar to touristic venues in Taksim. I used to dance in 7 or 8 different venues in one night.
- I danced at the wedding ceremony of a wedding contest TV show. Some people who watched me then, mentioned about me later. Mr. Ibrahim told them to find me and call me. His agent, Eyup Kanat, contacted me. When he said Mr. Ibrahim wanted to talk to me, I thought someone was pulling a joke on me. When we met, I was very excited and drenched in cold sweat. All of a sudden, I found myself in Ibo Show. I stand witness to how a person's life changes in one day. What I was yesterday, what I am today, what I will be tomorrow...
- I feel like the Snow White. Thank God. Thank God first, then thank Mr. Ibrahim. He is a person whose hands are to be kissed (an expression of respect and gratitude in Turkish culture; t.n.) In fact, even his feet can be kissed (an EXTREME form of expressing gratitude; t.n.) He's a boss who possesses and protects. I'm under protection even if I go to the other end of the world.
- I never thought of working for him but I dreamt of it. I used to loathe myself as nobody noticed me. When I went up on stage, audience used to talk to each other, never bothered to look at me. I used to close my eyes and say to myself: 'Help me, God, to take the stage in a beautiful place, where everyone would watch and applause me'

"It's hard not to talk"

- I try to distinguish my style from those of other belly dancers. I want to do Cha-Cha or Samba on the stage. I want to dance to the tunes of Indian music. My favorite is artistic gymnastics. Who knows, maybe if I did not drop out, I would be a gymnast one day.
- Mr. Ibrahim issued a talk-ban on me as he wanted the people to remember me by my dancing. In fact, it was good for me. Everybody was curious about me, asking 'Who's this girl, where's she from, who are her parents?'. When I went to Germany, people asked me if I was a deaf-mute. It's really hard not to talk at all. People rumoured about me, saying 'She can't speak Turkish, nor has she any manners'. I asked for Mr. Ibrahim's permission to prove them wrong, he kept saying 'All in good time...'

Later interview

Here is the belly dancer that will replace Asena!

Introducing his new partner for the first time in his live TV show, Ibrahim Tatlises said: "See how beautiful she is? I have an eye for the beauty anyway" -- Ibrahim Tatlises, whose both love and business partnership with Asena came to an abrupt ending, presented the belly dancer that will replace her the night before during the live broadcast of his TV show. Didem, who faced the live audience for the first time in her life with Ibo Show, will be a permanent element in all programmes of the famous singer.

Ibrahim Tatlises kept Asena by his side for many years. Asena was an integral part of his show during the concerts, stage shows and TV programmes. However, following a rather eventful ending of both their relationship and business partnership, Tatlises was looking for a new talent. The famous singer, who had been after a beautiful and talented belly dancer to replace Asena, finally found what he was looking for.

He conducted his search on his live 'Ibo Show', broadcast every Sunday on the Star TV channel, and even launched a minor contest. However, he finally picked up a divine beauty named Didem. He introduced the 20-year old beauty to the audience during his show for the first time. Tatlises, who introduced Didem during his show broadcast the night before, stated: "She will be the belly dancer of my show on a permanent basis. Besides, she will take the stage in Aso Bar at the summertime. See how beautiful she is? I have an eye for the beauty anyway."

Belly Dancer Didem: "My colleagues are envious and my parent are just exploiting me"

Belly Dancer Didem, whom Ibrahim Tatlises banned from speaking, finally broke her silence. She accused her colleagues of being jealous and spreading bad publicity about her, and complained that everybody around her changed all of a sudden when she became famous: 'Even my parents are exploiting me.'

Didem Kinali, the gorgeous and small belly dancer of Ibrahim Tatlises storms around on the stage in 'Ibo Show' each Sunday. 21 year old Roman girl greeted us in low-cut jeans, short t-shirt, canvas vest, a piercing on her belly button and braided hair, a sharp contrast with heavy make-up and belly-dance costumes, in which we were used to see her on TV...

"I'm a bit tactless"

She had a dog in her arms named 'Zeytin', which she found in the street. While she cleaned the dog's litter, she confided in us: "I hope Mr. Tatlises does not see this dog. He's already tired of the animals I found around"...

When we reminded her of the talk-ban, she replied: "To be honest, he has a point, as I'm a bit tactless". Though she chose all of her words very carefully during our interview, she also talked a storm as if to belie all those who claimed that 'she did not know how to talk'. Didem said that her biggest dream was to resume her education, which was cut short when she dropped out at the third grade.

- Were you a fan of Ibrahim Tatlises before you began working with him?

I usually listen to hip-hop, Western pop and rock music. I liked his songs as well but it never occurred to me that I might be working with him one day. When I received the offer, I first thought if it was a joke. Then asked myself if I was in a dream. I first confided in a very close girl friend. Told my mother three days later.

- Why you didn't share the news with your family first?

We were not in very good terms with my family. We were living separately anyway. I was earning my own money.

- Are you in better terms with your family now?

Yes, but we still are not living together.

- Is working with Mr. Tatlises hard or easy?

There are hard parts as well as easy parts. It's hard as I can't live my age.

But then, sometimes one has to make a sacrifice. He always gives me advise. Telling me to 'Keep your money, buy yourself a house, save it for the hard times, etc.'

- Do you heed his advice, then?

I just bought myself a car, not a house. I can't save much. I'm spending what I'm making (laughs)

- For how longer you will be talk-banned?

To be honest, it didn't start so it can't be over. It just developed spontaneously. I'm not a very talkative person. I feel stressed while talking next to a camera.

- Do you get excited?

I'm just afraid that I may say something wrong. I'm a little tactless (laughs)

"Too many people are jealous of me"

What are you going to say when you had a chance to speak for the first time? I'll let everyone know I'm a good person. Many people claimed so many things about me, some of which are real bad. This makes me sad.

- Don't you like to say something in defense?

No. I believe some people are a little perverted.

- Who do you think is promoting such derogations?

Definitely my colleagues. Probably out of jealousy.

- Did anyone else help you on your way to fame other than Mr. Tatlises?

Yes, Sema Yildiz, my belly-dance instructor. I met her when I was about 15. I started workin in the night clubs in Taksim. She spent a good deal of effort on me. I was very ignorant. Many bad things could have happened if it wasn't for her.

- Were or are there any belly dancers you perceive as your role model(s)?

I wanted to be another Tanyeli when I was a kid. However, I was not after fame. I just wanted to have a decent job.

"Everybody around me changed"

What has changed in your life when you became famous? I haven't changed but people around me have, and this includes my parents.

- For better or for worse?

Gee, honestly I don't know.

- Are you helping your family financially?

Yes. Sadly, they are exploiting me. I have a little problem about that (Didem's agent, who was present during the interview, prevented her to talk any further on this subject.)

- Are you still seeing your friends from your old neighborhood?

None left. All of them got married and had kids. Only I'm left.

- How do your fans react when they see you in public?

Honestly, they don't recognize me much. I wear hats to change my looks. In either case, I look very different on TV, taller, heavier.

- If you leave Mr. Tatlises one day, how would you like to live your life.

I'd love to stand on my own two feet! I always managed to accomplish some things on my own, and would like to go on this way.

"I'm in love with a dark, muscular sportsman"

- What about love?

Love... Nice name, but no presence of itself (laughs)

- You're still young and surely will love someone, someday...

I'm not saying I'm not in love. I love someone but he himself is not in my life (laughs)

- What do you mean? You're not together?

Yes, he's both in my life but at the same time, he isn't. Anyway, let's leave it as it is. Long story.

- What do you look for in a man?

I'm not considerin marriage but my boyfriend has to be honest with me. I do not tolerate a lie. He has to be interested in me as much as I'm interested in him. He shouldn't cheat on me. He should be very open with me and tell me if he doesn't like something directly to my face.

- What about physical attributes?

He must be dark and lean. I don't like stocky men. Must be a little muscular also. If I go on with the description, it will be too evident who he is (laughs)

- Oh, come on! More than half of the Turkish male population is dark and lean already (laughter)

For example, he must be a sportsman
- OK, so this 'nonexistent' lover is a sportsman (laughter)
I think I better shut up...

Source (edited): "http://en.wikipedia.org/wiki/Didem_(belly_dancer)"

Dina Talaat

Dina (Arabic: دينا) (born *Dina Talaat Sayed Mohamed*, IPA: [ˈdiːnæ ˈtˤalʕat ˈsæjjed mæˈħæmmæd]; 1964) is a leading Egyptian belly dancer and actress. She is one of the dancers who has a strong public presence.". She has a master's degree in Ancient Roman Theatre.

She was named as the "Last Egyptian Dancer" by the American magazine *Newsweek*.

Early life
She was born in Rome, Italy with her sister Rita, retired singer.

Filmography
- El-Kammasha (1987)
- En-Nasib Maktoub (1987)
- En-Nasib Maktoub (1987)
- Ginan fi Ginan (1990)
- Al-Ghashim (1991)
- Albaree wa al-Gallad (1991)
- Esteqalet Gaber (1992)
- Mazbahet al-Shorafaa (1992)
- Demo Sahebat Al-Galala (1992)
- Al-Mansi (1993) - **Guest of Honour**
- Qshr el-Bondoq (1995)
- Estakoza (1996)
- Ibn Ezz (2001)
- Alaya el-Tarab bet-Talata (2007)
- Elbelyatsho (2007)
- Maganin Nos Kom (2007)
- Ezbet Adam (2009)

Series
- Rod Qalbi (1998)
- Fereska (2004)
- Raya Wi Sekeena (2007)
- Romanet el-Mizan (2008)
- Al Ashrar (2009)
- Samasim (2009)
- Zahra Bareyya (2009)
- Khas Gedan (2009)
- Waad Mesh Maktoub (2009)

Theatre
- Alabanda (1995)

Source (edited): "http://en.wikipedia.org/wiki/Dina_Talaat"

Estelle Asmodelle

Estelle Asmodelle (born 22 April 1964, Bowral, New South Wales, Australia), formerly known as **Estelle Maria Croot**, is an Australian model, belly dancer, writer, musician and actress. She is known as Australia's first legal transsexual with the Births, Deaths and Marriages Department of New South Wales.

Estelle is an Australian transsexual who was instrumental in gaining recognition for transsexual and transgender people through her solo campaign to gain rights for transsexuals. In 1986, she was labelled "Australia's First Sex-Change Pin-up Girl". She is said to be the most photographed transsexual in Australia today.

Early life
Born in Bowral, and raised in Berrima, New South Wales, Estelle is the first child of Barry and Sylvia Croot. Her name at birth has not been disclosed. She has a sister, Belinda. She attended Chevalier College (then a boys-only school) and Moss Vale High School, where she frequently won first place in various subjects. When she was 16 years old she became seriously ill with spinal meningitis and spent almost one year in hospital. She used a wheelchair for some months and made a complete recovery.

After working briefly in Sydney, she moved to Wollongong and attended Wollongong University where she studied towards two degrees, a Bachelor of Science and a Bachelor of Mathematics, with the hope of becoming a research scientist. As a student she also worked in music ensembles, such as N-lettes and Miscellaneous Music composing and playing experimental and sometimes avant-garde musical art.

During the university period she experienced discrimination by members of the academic staff because of her transsexuality. For this reason, she left the University to focus on art and music. She became a dancer, believing that dance was the true artistic synthesis of art and music.

Dance career
After working briefly in Sydney as an assistant photographer, she attended dance classes at Sydney Dance Company and also with an Authentic Egyptian Dance instructor. Six weeks after starting belly dance classes she gained work as a dancer.

As time passed she worked in many shows both in Australia and Asia. She was typically featured as the variety act for such shows as Esma Duo, Paris by Night, Las Vegas Under Lights and Les Girls. She returned to Australia and worked as a solo belly dancer.

Activism
During Estelle's dance career she travelled to Asian countries and experienced many legal difficulties, especially in Singapore where she was detained, because her passport denoted an M (for male). She suffered serious problems with various customs officials and became determined to change the laws in Australia so as she could live as a normal woman. Australia's Department of Foreign Affairs and Trade policy was to issue passports bearing the gender designation F only to those transsexuals who could demonstrate that they had completed sex reassignment surgery.

Estelle continually sent letters and requests to the Attorney's General's Department of the Australian Government and eventually received confirmation that her requests were answered. Others had also been lobbying for changes; Roberta Perkins and Vivian Sharman, were two such activists, and had been lobbying the New South Wales government, especially the Attorney-General of N.S.W., for the right to amend birth certificates. Estelle was asked to go to the NSW Department of Births Deaths and Marriages and have her birth certificate amended. It was the first such amendment, making Estelle Asmodelle the first Legal Transsexual by recognition of the new name in the new gender. Months later, as a result of this action, passport sex designation was allowed to be amended as well. A year later Estelle lobbied for anti-discrimination laws to be amended and also for the state hospitals ethics boards to allow research into ectopic pregnancy for sex-change women.

Career

After a media storm during that period she decided to focus on her career. However her appearances were very extensive including hundreds of newspapers articles, and hundreds of magazine articles, including:
- *Cleo* (May 1987)
- *People* (Nov 1985 & 1993)
- *Post* (Dec 1988 Sep 1992)
- *Penthouse Forum* (1986 & 1991)
- *New Idea* (March 1986)
- *She* (July 1996)
- *New Woman* (June 1992 & 1998)
- *Naughty Sydney* (Cover – November 1991)
- *Tomadachi (June 1991)*
- *Wellbeing* (May 1989 & 1993)
- *Nature & Health (November 1997)*

She made more than 100 radio interviews and dozens of television appearances in Australia and Japan as well, including:
- *Where Are They Now?* (Channel 7)
- *Sex/Life* (Channel 10 TEN)
- *Midday Show with Kerri Anne* (Channel 9)
- *World View* (NHK Japan)
- *Beat Takeashi* (NHK Japan)
- *Good Morning Australia* (Channel 10)
- *Day by Day* (Channel 9)
- *Vox Populi* (SBS)
- *A Current Affair* (Channel 10)
- *Midday Show with Ray Martin* (Channel 9)
- *Terry Willisee|Terry Willisee Tonight* (Channel 9).

Film Work

After the media attention she garnered considerable publicity in Australia, but decided to live in Japan for a couple of years. It was there that she made her film debut, a walk in and walk out part, in a film by Japanese director Yoshimitsu Morita. It was made for the local Japanese market and never made it out of Japan. On returning to Australia, her next film was *The Enchanted Dance*, a documentary film about authentic belly dancing. It went international on video but was not released on DVD.

Filmography

Previous films:
- 1989 – *Ai to heisei no iro – Otoko*
- 1992 – *Secret Fantasies*
- 1994 – *The Enchanted Dance*

Current Productions
- 2011 – *The Edge of Fear*
- 2013 – *Pleasure Girl*

Modelling

Earlier on in her modelling career she became "Australia's First Transsexual Pin-up" by appearing nude in Australian Playgirl, unlike the US version of the magazine, the publication featured girls and not men, and it was the first time a transsexual had appeared in a mainstream magazine in Australia being nude. Estelle Asmodelle is also the face of the Supermodel Agency in Australia – she has been their spokesmodel and main model since 1996.

Currently

These days Asmodelle runs her network of modelling websites and now owns her own internet company, Ellenet Pty. Ltd. She has also acquired Night Star Pictures, an Australian film production company. According to media reports Estelle has become something of an internet entrepreneur and continues to build a significant online presence.

Music and writing

Estelle avoids media attention but models regularly and owns a small online modelling agency Australian Supermodel. She is working on her film career and hopes to launch her new cinema feature early 2009 as well a the proposed publishing of her Autobiographical novel, **Anaesthetic Dream**.

To date Estelle has written two books – which are still seeking publication:
- 2010 – *Anaesthetic Dream*
- 2009 – *Sex Business*

Estelle has a blog on one of her websites, namely; Asmodelle's Blog for updates on her activities. There is also an electronic music website that offers her electronic compositions as well (Asmodelle's Music).

To date Estelle has released 4 albums, which are available at iTunes, Amazon and most other online outlets, while her website also said they were released physically:
- 2009 – *Electronic Mischief*
- 2010 – *Transelectric*
- 2010 – *Dark Universe*
- 2011 – *Electrix*

Source (edited): "http://en.wikipedia.org/wiki/Estelle_Asmodelle"

Fifi Abdou

Fifi Abdou (Arabic: فيفي عبده) (born Atiyat Abdul Fattah Ibrahim; November 9, 1953) is a leading Egyptian belly dancer and actress. She has been described as "synonymous with belly dancing in the years she was performing."

In recent years, she has starred in several serial television dramas of the kind that are broadcast throughout the Arab world during Ramadan. In 2006, she took the lead in *Souq El Khudar* (*The

Greenmarket), playing a headstrong marketwoman with a love interest.

She married 5 times and has 2 daughters and currently her husbands the ambassador of Greenland).

Source (edited): "http://en.wikipedia.org/wiki/Fifi_Abdou"

Ghawazi

Photograph of a ghaziya (1906)

Lithograph by K. Craufurd (1880s)

Depiction of a ghaziya by Jean-Léon Gérôme (*L'Almée*, 1863).

Rotogravure of another depiction of a ghaziya by Gérôme

The **Ghawazi** (also *ghawazee*) dancers of Egypt were a group of female traveling dancers of the Nawari people, though some have erroneously associated them with the Dom people or "Gypsies".

The ghawazi style gave rise to the Egyptian raqs sharqi by the first half of the 20th century, and in turn to the Western forms of belly dance.

While the performative *raqs sharqi* in urban Egypt was heavily influenced by Western styles such as classical ballet or Latin American dance, the term *ghawazi* in Egypt refers to the dancers in rural Egypt who have preserved the traditional 18th to 19th century style.

Name

The Arabic غوازي *ghawāzī* (singular غازية *ghāziya*) means "conqueror", as the *ghaziya* is said to "conquer" the hearts of her audience. They were also known as *awālim* (singular *alma*, transliterated **almeh** in French as *almée*). Both terms are 19th-century euphemisms for "erotic dancer"; *almeh* literally means "learned woman" and came to be used as a replacement for *ghaziya* after the *ghawazi* were legally banned in 1834. An almeh in origin was a courtesan in Arab tradition, a woman educated to sing and recite classical poetry and to discourse. After the *ghawazi* were banned, they were forced to pretend that they were in fact *awalim*. The term *almeh* was introduced in French Orientalism as *almée* and used synonymously with "belly dancer".

History

In 1834s, the ghawazi were banished from Cairo to Upper Egypt by Muhammad Ali. Typically, the Ghawazi are represented as Gypsies, with a particular attention to their music and dance styles, featuring mizmars and heavy bass lines.

Beginning in the first half of the 19th century, descriptions and depictions of ghawazi dancers became famous in European Orientalism, and the style was described as *danse de ventre* or bellydance from the 1860s.

The Ghawazi performed unveiled in the streets. Rapid hip movement and use of brass hand castanets characterized their dance. Musicians of their tribe usually accompanied them in their dance. They usually wore kohl around their eyes and henna on their fingers, palms, toes and feet. According to Lane (1836) these women were "the most abandoned of the courtesans of Egypt". He describes them as being very beautiful and richly dressed.

The Ghawazi performed in the court of a house, or in the street, before the door, on certain occasions of festivity in the harem. They were never admitted into a respectable harem, but were frequently hired to entertain a party of men in the house of some rake. Both women and men enjoyed their entertainment. However, many people among the higher classes and more religious disapprove of them.

Many people liked the dancing of the Ghawazi, but felt it was improper because of its being danced by women who should not expose themselves in this manner. Because of this, there was a small number of young male performers called Khawals. The Khawals were Egyptian Muslims who impersonated the women of the Ghawazi and their dance. They were known to impersonate every aspect of the women including their dance and use of castanets.

Contemporary practitioners

Representing diverse historical backgrounds, most of the Ghawazi of the Qena region belong to ethnic minorities such as the Nawar (or Nawara), Halab, and Bahlawen.

Particularly well known are the Banat Maazin family, Nawar gypsys that settled in Luxor and were filmed in the 70's and 80's. Many consider the Maazin family to be the only practicing family left of the original line of Ghawazi dancers.

Influence on western belly-dance

The style of dance and costuming of the Ghawazi has been especially influential in crafting the look of American Tribal Style Belly Dance. Traditional Ghawazi dress consists of an Ottoman coat with slits, known as a Yelek or entari. The abdomen is covered by these coats. Turkish harem pants are worn under these coats. The coats are typically ankle-length, though some modern Ghawazee troupes wear a shorter version over a full, knee-length skirt. Ghawazee dancers often adorn their heads with elaborate headresses, with dancers often accompanying themselves by playing zils, or small cymbals that are used by dancers in many forms of Oriental dance.

Source (edited): "http://en.wikipedia.org/wiki/Ghawazi"

Maria Jammal

Maria Jammal is a Moroccan bellydance choreographer noted for incorporating ballet and bellydance. Maria was born and raised in Casablanca, Morocco, she studied ballet since the age of eight. She went on to explore Jazz, Modern and contemporary styles.

At 18 she won first place at the Conservatoire Casablanca and was given a scholarship at the Paris Opera. At twenty-one, she moved to Paris to continue her dance studies and perform with the Paris Opera School of Ballet. She lived in France for 12 years.

She traveled to Egypt to study Oriental dance, then opened her own school in Casablanca in 1986. She has danced for both the Rothschild and Saudi Arabian royal families.

Maria married her Lebanese husband, and now they have two children, a boy and a girl, Mohamad Jammal and Sarah Jammal. Maria has also performed in several films and television programs in both Morocco and Egypt.

Source (edited): "http://en.wikipedia.org/wiki/Maria_Jammal"

Nadia Gamal

Nadia Gamal (Arabic: نادية جمال) was an Egyptian dancer and actress. She is often credited as the originator of the modern style of Lebanese raqs sharqi, or belly dance.

Early life and career

Born as **Maria Carydias** to a Greek father and an Italian mother in Alexandria, Egypt, Gamal first began dancing as a part of her mother's cabaret act. Trained in piano as well as several kinds of dance such as ballet and tap, Gamal initially performed European folk dances in her mother's act. When she was 14, an ill dancer in her mother's troupe gave her the opportunity to dance raqs sharqi in Lebanon, which her father had forbidden her to do because of her youth. After this debut, she became a popular dancer and went on to star in many Egyptian films.

In 1968, Gamal became the first raqs sharqi dancer to perform at the Baalbeck International Festival. She also appeared at the Cairo Opera House and danced for King Hussein and the Shah of Iran. Gamal toured Asia, the Middle East, Europe, Latin America and North America during her career. In 1978 and 1981 she briefly taught dance workshops in New York City. Later in her career, Gamal started a school of dance.

Gamal was diagnosed with breast cancer in 1990, and while undergoing treatment in Beirut contracted pneumonia and died.

Style and influence

Gamal was known for her extensive use of floorwork. She also often included raqs baladi (folkloric dance), Bedouin dances and Zār dance with raqs sharqi in her performances.

She influenced many dancers such as Ibrahim Farrah, Suhaila Salimpur, and Claire Naffa.

Filmography

- *Prem Pujari* (1970)
- *Bazi-e eshgh* (1968)
- *Bazy-e-shance* (1968)
- *Mawal al akdam al zahabiya* (1966)
- *Twenty-Four Hours to Kill* (1965)
- *Garo* (1965)
- *Layali al chark* (1965)
- *Zenubba* (1956)
- *Mawwal*

Source (edited): "http://en.wikipedia.org/wiki/Nadia_Gamal"

Nagwa Fouad

Nagwa Fouad (Arabic: نجوى فؤاد, Egyptian Arabic: [ˈnæɡwæ foˈʔæːd]; born 1943) is a famous Egyptian belly dancer.

After her release she performed at the Abdeen Casino where she met Ahmad Fuad Hassan (her future husband for 6 years), a producer of stage shows that later became a famous conductor. He convinced her to perform live at the most prestigious music and dance show in the 1960s called Adwa El Madina (City Lights) which had featured such superstars as Shadia, Abdel Halim Hafez, Fayza Ahmed, and Sabah.

In 1976, the famous composer Mohammed Abdel Wahab wrote an entire musical piece exclusively for her belly dancing show titled Qamar Arba'tashar (meaning the full Moon of the 14th), it was her transition from traditional oriental dance to a choreographed stage performances.

The next important career step was Nagwa's marriage to Ahmed Fouad Hassan, the talented violin player, composer and conductor. Ahmed gave Nagwa Fouad her chance to appear in the very popular sixties stage show "Adwoua Al-Madina" (City Lights), which had featured such superstars as Abdel-Halim Hafez, Fayza Ahmed, Shadia and Sabah. Nagwa featured on many of the covers of the Ahmed Fouad Hassan LP's/CD's. Nagua took every career step well calculated: "Hassan was 17 years older than me, but I needed him. He nurtured my amateur's talents... He taught me the importance of studying and working on my talent if I wanted to be a big star. He trained me at the Nelly Mazloum Dance School and I joined the National Dance Troupe to study folklore with Russian teachers." Nagoua Fouad learned showmanship and eye-catching techniques which were obvious in her performances of "Ayoub Al-Masri" and "Bahiya wa Yassin". But Fouad Hassan wanted to have a baby with Nagua. Something she didn't approve to so this eventually led to her first divorce after six years of marriage. In 1976, Nagwa Fouad reached the top of her career when composer Mohamed Abdel-Wahab wrote "Qamar Arbaatashar" (Blue Moon or 14the moon) for her. Her stage performance to this special piece allowed her to change the way belly-dancing was presented on stage, transforming it from traditional oriental dance to more of a choreographed lavish spectacle adding more dramatic elements to it than ever before. The composition served as a transition for Nagwa: "I was able to combine the oriental dancing of Tahiya Karioka and Samia Gamal with Na'ema's acrobatic style and created a stage show like a dramatic piece" she says. Najwa established her own dance group but it did not last long and later tried to retire dancing to become actress. She played on the stage and in the cinema and finally became cinema producer.

Famous performances

- Qamar Arba'tashar (Moon of the 14th) 1976
- Music by Mohammed Abdel Wahab

Source (edited): "http://en.wikipedia.org/wiki/Nagwa_Fouad"

Naima Akef

Naima Akef (Arabic: نعيمة عاكف, 7 October 1929 - 23 April 1966) was a famous Egyptian belly dancer during the Egyptian cinema's golden age and starred in many films of the time. Naima Akef was born in Tanta on the Nile Delta. Her parents were acrobats in the Akef Circus (run by Naima's grandfather), which was one of the best known circuses at the time. She started performing in the circus at the age of four, and quickly became one of the most popular acts with her acrobatic skills. Her family was based in the Bab el Khalq district of Cairo, but they traveled far and wide in order to perform.

Dancing

The circus disbanded when Naima was 14, but this was only the beginning of her career. Her grandfather had many connections in the performance world of Cairo and he introduced her to his friends. When Naima's parents divorced, she formed an acrobatic and clown act that performed in many clubs throughout Cairo. She then got the chance to work in Badeia Masabny's famous nightclub, where she became a star and was one of the very few who danced and sang. Her time with Badeia, however, was short-lived, as Badeia favored her, which made the other performers jealous. One day they ganged up on her and attempted to beat her up, but she proved to be stronger and more agile and won the fight. This caused her to be fired, so she started performing elsewhere.

A star

The Kit Kat club was another famous venue in Cairo, and this is where Naima was introduced to film director Abbas Kemal. His brother Hussein Fawzy, also a film director, was very interested in having Naima star in one of his musical films. The first of such films was "Al-Eïch wal malh" (bread and salt). Her costar was singer Saad Abdel Wahab, the nephew of the legendary singer and composer Mohammed Abdel Wahab. The film premiered on the 17th of January 1949, and was an instant success, bringing recognition also to Nahhas Film studios.

Retirement and death

Naima quit acting in 1964 to take care of her only child, a son from her second marriage to accountant Salaheldeen Abdel Aleem. She died two years later from cancer, on April 23, 1966, at the age of 36.

Filmography

- Aish Wal Malh (1949).
- Lahalibo (1949).
- Baladi Wa Khafa (1949).
- Furigat (1950).
- Baba Areess (1950).
- Fataat Al Sirk (1951).
- Ya Halawaat Al Hubb (1952).
- Arbah Banat Wa Zabit (1954).
- Aziza (1955).
- Tamr Henna (1957). with Ahmed Ramzy, Fayza Ahmed and Rushdy Abaza.
- Amir El Dahaa (1964).

Source (edited): "http://en.wikipedia.org/wiki/Naima_Akef"

Nejla Ates

Nejla Ates was a Turkish belly dancer and actress born in 1933. Notably, she appeared the film *Son of Sinbad* and *Fanny*, a Broadway musical.

There was a statue of her in Central Park in November 1954 (as a publicity stunt). *Glamour Girls of the Silver Screen* states that she was born in Romania on 7 March 1932 and died in Istanbul in April 2005.

Source (edited): "http://en.wikipedia.org/wiki/Nejla_Ates"

Nelly Mazloum

Nelly Mazloum (1929 - 21 February 2003) was an Egyptian actress, dancer and choreographer of Greek origin who taught ballet, modern dance, folkloric Egyptian dances and artistic oriental dance. Known for her sense of humor, she is famous for her role in the movie *Ibn Hamidu* along with Ismail Yasseen.

The early years

Nelly-Catherine Mazloum-Calvo was born in Alexandria, Egypt into a Greek family. Her father was an Italian from Naples and her mother a Greek from Asia Minor. Her father created costume jewellery and her mother was an able pianist. They owned a hotel across the street from the Alambra theatre. Mazloum suffered from paralysis of the legs at the age of two and walked again after years of loving care by a paediatrician and his wife, a ballet teacher. That's where she learned to dance.

At the age of five, she auditioned at the theatre and started a dance career as a child prodigy, from 1939 to 1945, working in two shows a day, all year: in Alexandria in the summer months, in Cairo during the winter, the darling of the elite society. She danced at the famous Opera Casino, run by Badya Masabni, where oriental dance greats started. There were two shows: a matinee, for families, which ended at eight o'clock (and where Nelly danced, always under the watchful eyes of her mother, who was her shrewd impresario), and then the other one, where spirits were served. The little girl, once her own dancing was over, stayed on to watch the rehearsal of the great artists such as Samia Gamal and Tahiya Karioka, directed by an Italian choreographer, who would create special moves for them. She appeared in front of King Farouk, in the same show as Samia Gamal and Umm Kulthum. Most of the time she danced ballet or modern dance.

In 1939 the 10-year-old Mazloum appeared on her first film, *I prosfygopoula* (The refugee girl), a Greek language movie starring Sophia Vembo, on a screenplay by D. Bogris, followed in 1940 by *Ben Nareen*.

The golden years

In the 1940s and 50s the strikingly beautiful young woman danced in all the choicest venues, creating her own choreographies, and as an actress in the theatre and in the cinema, for about 17 films. Of those, she performed oriental dance only in two. One is *Shahrazad* (1941) starring Hussein Sedky, Elham Hussein and Samia Gamal, the other one was *Soliman's Ring* (1946), directed by Hassan Ramzy (the uncle of percussionist Hossam Ramzy). Simone Gasser (Meissoun), a Swiss oriental dancer who took seminars with her, says: "According to her, the reason why she didn't do Raqs Sharqi in films was because 'everybody else did it' and they wanted her to do other dances because she could." According to Mazloum's daughter Marianna, "There were some 300 Egyptian dancers doing oriental very cheaply, they could be hired for 5 pounds per film, while my mother commanded a hefty cachet of 100 pounds because she was the only modern dancer in Egypt at that time — so why 'waste' her on something everybody else did?" She also ran a successful ballet school, which provided young artists for the National Opera of Cairo.

Nelly liked the luxuries in life, and she enjoyed life to the full. She was married six times. One of her husbands was a Greek-Egyptian named Andreas Roussos (unrelated to engineer Yorgos Roussos, the father of (Demis Roussos). She was married to him for four years, and he was the father of her two children: Emanuel and, two years later, Marianna (also known by her pet name and stage name Marhaba). Marianna says:
My father was very rich, the owner of a candy factory. He didn't want my mother to dance, so she stopped performing and concentrated on research. Although her main training was in ballet, she never missed a chance to learn Egyptian dance forms. When I was small I remember we visited my father's sweet factory and when there was a festivity, we watched the girls dance to music from the radio. Outside the building there was a cul-de-sac where these poor people always held their weddings, borrowing the tables from the factory.Moreover, she took the car and chauffeur and went around to watch people in their original surroundings, Bedouin marriages in the desert etc... She traveled the whole country for many years, from the desert to the villages, souks, cities, always looking for new dance movements.During her visits to the rich Egyptian ladies, on the other hand, she would watch their dance too: a different sort of dance, more refined than the beledi or the shaabi - she calls it hawanem. She absorbed it all. An avid reader, she never visited a bookstore without coming home with 30-40 books. She once took a whole year to study books in the National Egyptian Museum, looking for descriptions of dances and costumes in ancient times. The director gave her a special permission, and she had to handle the fragile manuscripts with gloves.

The Nelly Mazloum troupe
Eventually, Mazloum divorced her husband, opened a ballet school, and returned to performing, ready to form her own dance company. The members were all amateurs, some taken from her ballet school, some from the field of gymnastics, some were students and some had another morning job. After two years of hard work, they staged, in 1956 (three years before the creation of the Mahmoud Reda troupe), a show with Egyptian folklore, the first of its kind. Her troupe started with 25 people but soon grew to 40 dancers (20 female and 20 male) with a 50-people orchestra. The dance style she called Raqs el Ta'biri (Expressive Dancing) and was her own artistic elaboration and stylization of the raw material of folk dances she had seen and studied. The programme included scenes from rural life. By then she had started dancing again and took part in the performances. Now her school had two branches, the ballet school (for the girls of the elite society) and the folkloric school, for the training of company members. Marianna Mazloum said:
The company presented only the folkloric style of dance. Raqs Sharqi was not considered worthy of the stage, at those times, it was only done in nightclubs or in parties. As for Raqs el Hawanem it was done inside the homes. There was no company in Egypt which presented oriental dance on the stage.
They performed in high-end venues like the Montaza Gardens. In 1958, the company was showcased in the great International Fair for Egyptian Cotton, at the Grand Palais in Gezira, and won more and more acclaim, as testified by numerous newspaper articles.

In 1959, Mahmoud Reda, his brother Ali Reda and his sister-in-law Farida Fahmy co-founded the Reda Troupe. It is unclear why some of their collaborators, such as Atef Farag, claim to be the first to present folkloric dances in the theatre and to be "the first Egyptian dance company to record Egyptian folk songs and dances from many different and remote regions of Egypt and perform them on stage."

In 1959-60, the Egyptian government wanted to establish a National Ballet Academy and called Mr. Jukov, assistant teacher at the Bolshoi Ballet in the then Soviet Union, to help. Mazloum was chosen as his assistant, for her knowledge of classical dance and Arabic. For three years she was his right hand. The next year, another ambitious project was formed: the establishment of a National Folkloric Academy and yet another Russian, Mr. Ramazen, came for that purpose. Again Mazloum was his bridge to the local talent. He came to her in the morning to learn the movements of folkloric dances which he then showed to the dancers in the afternoon. However, when she saw that the Russians adulterated the Egyptian style and made it more Russian, she quit the job. But her experience with them was invaluable, helping her to organize her knowledge of technique and create a method for her own school — what would emerge as her signature style.

It was a time of great political favour. The Minister of Culture, Dr. Sarwat Okasha, was so enthusiastic about her work that he used to buy tickets for poor people to see her shows without paying. In 1961, he gave the company a floating theatre, a boat, which toured the Nile back and forth, stopping to perform at every village. Mazloum also did experimental styles like pharaonic dance (she presented it at the first 'Sound and light' show), a "desert dance" with veil, etc. One of her great successes was the biblical story *Ayub el Masri*, in 1962. It was also the year she and her company participated in the Helsinki International-al Youth Festival, where she was awarded the Silver Medal for her folkloric dances *Al Ghazl*, representing the weaving of the bridal veil. She became the official choreographer of the Cairo Opera, for opera and operetta productions. She choreographed, among others, *Mahr el Aroussa* (The bride's dowry) in 1963, the first all-Arabic classical operetta.

After having formed the Ballet Academy and the Folkloric Dance Academy, the government approached her about forming a National Folklore troupe (without her). She replied "the troupe without me does not exist" and refused, remaining independent. Mahmoud Reda's troupe became the National Troupe.

The move to Greece

In 1964 the government changed, and the minister of culture fell in disgrace, with all his proteges. Most of Mazloum's dancers were lured to the National Reda company, with a higher pay. The new people in favour made life for Mazloum very difficult, starting a slander campaign in the press. She packed all her belongings, put her children temporarily in a boarding school, and left Egypt for Greece, starting afresh. There, she buried all the tokens of her past career in a series of trunks and vowed never to dance again, but concentrate on teaching and propagating the art of dance, founding the Athens International School where, again, she taught ballet and modern dance. She changed her name to Nelly M. Calvo, so that people wouldn't associate her with her past self.

Teaching dance and the MADRI foundation

From 1985 she restarted teaching oriental dance, creating the Nelly Mazloum Oriental Dance Technique (1988), which includes her own signature style, called ["Hawanem"] the dance of high nobility which she was the first to introduce in Europe and has become her signature style. She also started giving a series of seminars abroad, fighting to ban the word "bellydance" in favour of "oriental dance". She also developed her own system of working out, called the Vivicorporeal Psychosomatic Alignment Technique, to support Oriental dance.

In 1990 she wrote *Oriental Dance Technique* (1992) and in 2001 she founded the Nelly Mazloum Mediterranean Archaic Dances Research Institute (MADRI), a nonprofit organization aiming at evolution and preservation of Mediterranean Archaic Dances As Mazloum wrote: "Archaic Dances still influence our moving center for they are rooted in the cosmic memory of our planet. They may disappear into the past but always find their way back to us through research work & Spiritual Identification."

She died on 21 February 2003.

Her daughter, Marianna Roussou Mazloum, has continued teaching the traditional Nelly Mazloum Oriental dance technique as well as Vivicorporeal classes and has continued in her role as the co-founder of MADRI in Athens, Greece. The Madri Institute organizes classes and seminars on the Nelly Mazloum Oriental Dance Technique and Vivicorporeal, in Athens and abroad.
Source (edited): "http://en.wikipedia.org/wiki/Nelly_Mazloum"

Rachel Brice

Rachel Brice is a contemporary innovator in Tribal Fusion Style Belly Dance based in San Francisco. She is the artistic director and choreographer for The Indigo Belly Dance Company and a frequent performer with the Bellydance Superstars.

She has performed and toured nationally and internationally since 1990. As a member of the Bellydance Superstars Brice made numerous appearances on Bellydance Superstars DVDs, as well as a multitude of television and radio appearances worldwide, most notably Live with Regis and Kelly in the US and Blue Peter in England.

As a teacher and movement arts pedagogue, Brice has released instructional videos focusing on Yoga and Belly Dance, and has given workshops throughout the United States and Europe. Brice also teaches Yoga and Belly Dance for Pixar Animation Studios.

From Brice's website:
"Rachel Brice first fell in love with Belly Dance after watching the famous Hahbi'Ru at the Northern California Renaissance Faire in 1988 and began taking classes right away. In 1999, she decided to study full time, and relocated for the University program in Dance Ethnology at San Francisco State University. In 2003 she was discovered by rock mogul Miles Copeland and began touring internationally with his company, Bellydance Superstars. Also in 2003 she founded The Indigo Belly Dance Company. 2007 marks The Indigo's first full-length touring show, Le Serpent Rouge, presented by Miles Copeland. When home, Rachel studies Belly Dance with her teachers Suhaila Salimpour, and creator of American Tribal Style, Carolena Nericcio, and Yoga with Gary Kraftsow."

Filmography

Performance

- "Bellydance Superstars Live in Paris: Folies Bergeres"
- "Bellydance Superstars Solos in Monte Carlo"
- "Bellydance Superstars"

Instructional

- "Tribal Fusion: Yoga, Isolations and Drills a Practice Companion with Rachel Brice"
- "Rachel Brice: Belly Dance Arms and Posture"
- "SERPENTINE: With World Dance New York"

Musical collaborations

- "Sa'iyr - A Tribal Metamorphosis" (2005) - Pentaphobe (also known as "A Tribal Metamorphosis")
- "Bellydance Superstars volume 1" -

Musical Selection
- "Bellydance Superstars volume 2" - Musical Selection
- "Bellydance Superstars volume 3" - Musical Selection
- "Le Serpent Rouge: Musical Selections from the Knockdown Revue" - Compilation

Source (edited): "http://en.wikipedia.org/wiki/Rachel_Brice"

Rozeta Ahalyea

Rozeta Ahalyea was one of the earliest professional bellydancers in Australia with a performance career that spanned four decades. She trained Amera Eid and Terezka Drznik, who both became distinguished teachers and who themselves taught many of today's professional Australian belly dancers. In this regard, although not enjoying great fame during her career, she is an important figures in Australian belly dance history

Born in Greece and emigrating to Australia in the early 1950s, Ahalyea's professional career started in 1962 at age 16, arriving in Sydney after running away from home to escape an arranged marriage. Rozeta found work as a cashier in a Spanish nightclub in Kings Cross and this is where she saw her first bellydancer. The boss of the nightclub overheard her boasting she could dance better than the dancer on stage. He found Rozeta a costume and she performed for the first time doing a Greek Tsifteteli that she had learnt growing up, with an accompanying live band. The crowd enjoyed the performance so much the boss gave her a job as a full time dancer.

Six months later she toured Japan for six months and at the age of 17 was the youngest solo artist ever to visit. She then moved to Hong Kong for 3 months before going to Thailand.

Unbeknown to Rozeta the owner of the Thai nightclub she was contracted to was the Prince of Thailand. After a month long courtship they became engaged. Their engagement broke down upon learning that the Prince wanted more than one wife, as was custom in Thai tradition. She fled the country with the help of a General's wife, who was British, via Hong Kong and Taiwan before returning to Australia. She waited until she qualified for an Australian passport before working overseas again.

Rozeta worked extensively in the Sydney restaurant and nightclub scene but due to ill health from the smoky environment she moved to Queensland.

While in Australia, she also taught bellydancing privately. Two notable students were Amera Eid who eventually set up Amera's Palace, the first bellydance boutique in Australia, and Terezka Drnzik who started Sydney's first full time bellydance school.

Source (edited): "http://en.wikipedia.org/wiki/Rozeta_Ahalyea"

Samia Gamal

Samia Gamal (Arabic: سامية جمال), born as **Zaynab Ibrahim Mahfuz**), (February 22, 1922 - December 1, 1994) was an Egyptian belly dancer and film actress.

Born in the small Egyptian town of Wana in 1924, Samia's family moved just months later to Cairo and settled near the Khan El-Khalili bazaar. It was many years later that Samia Gamal met Badia Masabni, the founder of modern Oriental dance. Badia offered Samia an invitation to join her dance company, which Samia accepted. Badia Masabni gave her the stage name Samia Gamal, and she began her dance career.

Samia Gamal and Farid Al-Attrach in the Egyptian movie Afrita Hanem *(Genie Lady)* (1947)

At first, she studied under Badia and Badia's star dancer at the time, Tahiya Karioka. However she soon became a respected soloist and brought forth her own style. Samia Gamal incorporated techniques from ballet and Latin dance into her solo performances. She was also the first to perform with high-heeled shoes on stage. She starred in dozens of Egyptian films next to the famous Farid Al Attrach. They could be easily thought of as the Fred Astaire and Ginger Rogers of the Middle East. They not only played each others' love interest on the silver screen but also in real life. However, their love was not meant to be. Because of Farid's social position, he refused to marry Samia. Farid believed that marriage kills artist talent, he never got married until he died. Some claim that Farid as a Druze prince, told her it would bring too much shame to his family for him to marry a belly dancer. But that claim is baseless. Farid helped placing Samia on the National Stage by risking all he owned, and managed to borrow to produce a movie (Habib al omr) co-starring with her in 1947. In 1949, Egypt's King Farouk proclaimed Samia Gamal "The National Dancer of Egypt", which brought US attention to the dancer.

In 1950, Samia came to the US and was photographed by Gjon Mili. She also performed in Latin Quarter (nightclub), New York's trendy nightclub. She later married so-called "Texas millionaire" Shepherd King III (who, it was later reported, actually only had about $50,000). All this brought her to star proportions in the US.

However, their marriage didn't last long. In 1958, Samia Gamal married Roshdy Abaza, one of the most famous Egyptian actors with whom Samia starred in a number of movies as well. Samia Gamal stopped dancing in 1972 when she was nearly in her 50s but began again after given advice by Samir Sabri. She then danced until the early 1980s.

Samia Gamal died on December 1, 1994, at 72 years of age in Cairo, Egypt. Samia's charismatic performances in Egyptian and international films gave Oriental Dance recognition and admiration in Egypt and worldwide. She was and still is deeply mourned by the dance community.

Filmography

- *Samia Forever (Documentary, 2003)*
- *Fabulous Samia Gamal, The, (Documentary, 2003)*
- *The Stars of Egypt: Volume 3: Samia Gamal, Part I (Film, 19??)*
- *The Stars of Egypt: Volume 3: Samia Gamal, Part II (Film, 19??)*
- *Tarik al shaitan...aka The Way of the Devil (Film, 1963)*
- *Waada el hub... aka And Love Returned (Film, 1961)*
- *Nagham el hazine, El... aka Sad Melody (Film, 1960)*
- *Rajul el thani, El... aka The Second Man (Film, 1960)*
- *Kull daqqa fi qalbi... aka Every Beat of My Heart (Film, 1959)*
- *Maweed maa maghoul... aka Rendezvous with a Stranger (Film, 1959)*
- *Gharam al-miliunayr aka Love of the Millionaire (Film, 1957)*
- *Amanti del deserto, Gli...aka Desert Warrior (Film, 1956)*
- *Masque de Toutankhamon, Le...aka Trésor des pharaons, Le (Film, 1955)*
- *Sigarah wa kas... aka A Cigarette and a Glass (Film, 1955)*
- *Ali Baba et les quarante voleurs...aka Ali Baba; Ali Baba and the Forty Thieves (Film, 1954)*
- *Valley of the Kings* (Film, 1954)
- *Nachala hanem... aka The Lady Pickpocket (Film, 1954)*
- *Raqsat al-wadah... aka The Farewell Dance (Film, 1954)*
- *El Wahsh... aka The Monster (Film, 1954)*
- *Ketar el lail... aka The Night Train (Film, 1953)*
- *Ma takulshi la hada... aka Tell No-one; Don't Tell Anyone (Film, 1952)*
- *Amir el antikam... aka The Count of Monte Cristo (Film, 1951)*
- *Taa la salim... aka Come and Say Hello (Film, 1951)*
- *Ahmar shafayef... aka Lipstick (Film, 1950)*
- *Akher kedba... aka The Final Lie (Film, 1950)*
- *Sakr, El... aka The Falcon (Film, 1950)*
- *Nuit des étoiles, La (Film, 1950)*
- *Agaza fel gahannam... aka Holidays in Hell (Film, 1949)*
- *Bahebbak inta... aka I Love You Only (Film, 1949)*
- *Bint haz... aka The Lucky Girl (Film, 1949)*
- *Sparviero del Nilo, Lo (Film, 1949)*
- *Mughamer, El... aka The Adventurer (Film, 1948)*
- *Sahibat el amara... aka The Landlady (Film, 1948)*
- *Afrita hanem... aka Lady Afrita; Lady Genie; Little Miss Devil; The Genie Lady (Film, 1947)*
- *Ahdab, El... aka The Hunchback (Film, 1947)*
- *Ersane talata, El... aka The Three Suitors (Film, 1947)*
- *Habib al omr... aka The Love of My Life (Film, 1947)*
- *Bani adam, al-... aka Sons of Adam (Film, 1945)*
- *Taxi hantur... aka A Hansom Carriage (Film, 1945)*
- *Russassa fil kalb... aka A Bullet in the Heart (Film, 1944)*
- *Ali Baba wa al arbain harame... aka Ali Baba and the Forty Thieves (Film, 1942)*
- *Gawhara (Film, 1942)*

Source (edited): "http://en.wikipedia.org/wiki/Samia_Gamal"

Serena Wilson

Serena Wilson (August 8, 1933 – June 17, 2007), often known just as "Serena", was a well-known dancer, choreographer, and teacher who helped popularize belly dance in the United States. Serena's work also helped legitimize the dance form and helped it to be perceived as more than burlesque or stripping. Serena danced in clubs in her younger years, opened her own studio, hosted her own television show, founded her own dance troupe, and was the author of several books about belly dance.

Early years

Serena was born Serene Blake in 1933 in New York's Bronx. Her parents were vaudeville performers with their own show, Blake & Blake, featuring a variety of comedy and musical numbers, some of which Serena performed in as a child. As a young adult, Serena officially changed her name from "Serene" to "Serena".

Serena also began studying with famed dancer Ruth St. Denis, well-known for her interpretations of Oriental and Oriental-style dance. In 1952, Serena married Alan (Rip) Wilson, a musician, percussionist, and leader of a Dixieland band, a combination which complemented Serena's own background. In the mid-1950s, Serena gave birth to their son, Scott.

Not long after their marriage, Rip's band was booked for a gig with a Middle Eastern theme that required a belly dancer. In spite of the clash of styles, Rip quickly got hold of the music for popular Middle Eastern standards like Misirlou, and recruited his wife to dance, which Serena felt her studies with St. Denis had prepared her for.

According to her husband, Serena's dance ended up being rather awkward, as she wasn't sure what to do with her hands. She disguised this by carrying a vase on her shoulder throughout! The performance was nonetheless a success, inspiring Serena and Rip to pursue a life-long interest in Middle Eastern music and dance.

Rip took up Middle Eastern drumming and frequently accompanied Serena as she honed her skills dancing at the Egyptian Gardens club in Chelsea, an area then known colloquially as Greektown for the large number of Greek and Middle Eastern cabarets lining the street. Soon, Serena had become one of the most popular belly dancers in the city and even performed for various city officials.

Middle years

In the mid-1960s, Serena began teaching belly dance, opening Serena Studios, on Eighth Avenue in New York City. In the 1970s she started her own TV show, known as *Serena* and *The Serena Show*, which served as a means of educating the masses about belly dancing and billed itself as "The fun way to beauty, grace, and a youthful figure."

Her son, Scott, continued the family tradition by dedicating himself to the study of the oud, an Egyptian lute or guitar. Serena began writing the first two of her books about belly dance, *The Serena Technique of Belly Dancing* and *The Belly Dance Book*.

Serena and Rip's success continued unabated until the Gulf War in 1991, when American attitudes toward all things Middle Eastern soured.

Later years

In spite of the bias in American popular culture against the Middle East, Serena continued to perform in a number of Egyptian folkloric shows and appeared several times as the lead dancer in the New York Opera Company's production of *Aida*. She also continued teaching at her studio and choreographing for her troupe, Serena Dance Theater, which performed throughout New York City.

Serena's studio provided dancers for hire, with dancers available for performances at traditional Middle Eastern weddings and other social events. Notably, in keeping with Serena's long-held belief that belly dancing was not comparable with stripping and erotic dance, her studio would not provide dancers for events in which their performance might be over-sexualized, e.g., for bachelorette parties but not bachelor parties, for bat mitzvahs but not bar mitzvahs.

In June 2007, Serena died suddenly of a pulmonary embolism. She had been scheduled to dance in Greenwich Village with her son's Middle Eastern band, Scott Wilson and Efendi, that very night. Her son and husband continue to carry on her passion for Middle Eastern music and dance. Serena's studio in New York continues to hold classes and provide dancers for performances.

Source (edited): "http://en.wikipedia.org/wiki/Serena_Wilson"

Shakira

Shakira Isabel Mebarak Ripoll (born February 2, 1977), known professionally as **Shakira** (pronounced /ʃəˈkɪɹəɹə/, Spanish: [tʃaˈkira] or [ʃaˈkiɾa]), is a Colombian singer, songwriter, musician, record producer, dancer, and philanthropist who emerged in the music scene of Colombia and Latin America in the early 1990s. Born and raised in Barranquilla, Colombia, Shakira revealed many of her talents in school as a live performer, demonstrating her vocal ability with rock and roll, Latin and Middle Eastern influences with her own original twist on belly dancing. Shakira is a native Spanish speaker and also speaks fluent English and Portuguese as well as some Italian, French and Arabic.

After commercial flops with local producers on her first two albums, and being little-known outside Colombia, Shakira decided to produce her own brand of music. In 1995 she released *Pies Descalzos*, which brought her great fame in Latin America and Spain, and her 1998 album *¿Dónde Están los Ladrones?* was a critical success selling over 7 million copies worldwide. In 2001, aided by the worldwide success of her first English single "Whenever, Wherever" that became the best selling single of 2002, she broke through into the English-speaking world with the release of *Laundry Service*, which sold over 13 million copies worldwide. Four years later, Shakira released two album projects called *Fijación Oral Vol. 1* and *Oral Fixation Vol. 2*. Both reinforced her success, particularly with the best selling song of the 2000s, "Hips Don't Lie".

In 1995, Shakira founded the Pies Descalzos Foundation. It is a Colombian charity with special schools for poor children all around Colombia. During her career, Shakira has performed at a large number of benefit concerts. Among the most famous are the Live 8 benefit concert in July 2005, the Live Earth concert, Hamburg where she headlined the show, as well as the "Clinton Global Initiative" created by former US President Bill Clinton. She was also invited to the Oval Office by President Barack Obama in February 2010 to discuss early childhood development.

She has won two Grammy Awards, seven Latin Grammy Awards, twelve Billboard Latin Music Awards and has been Golden Globe-nominated. She is also the highest-selling Colombian artist of all time, and the second most successful female Latin singer after Gloria Estefan, having sold over 50 million albums worldwide according to Sony Music Entertainment. Her U.S. album sales stand at 9.6 million.

In the fall of 2009, Shakira released her sixth album *She Wolf* worldwide. Shakira's "Waka Waka (This Time for Africa)", was chosen as the official song for the 2010 FIFA World Cup. The song has received generally positive critical reception, and has become a worldwide smash hit and the biggest selling World Cup song of all time. On YouTube, the English version of the music video is the 3rd most watched video of all time with over 300 million views. Her seventh studio album, the bilingual *Sale el Sol*, was released October 2010 and has shipped over 4 million copies worldwide.

She was engaged to the son of the former President of Argentina, Antonio de la Rúa. Their relationship lasted almost 11 years and ended in August 2010. She is now dating Spanish footballer Gerard Piqué and confirmed their relationship in March 2011.

Early life

Shakira was born on February 2, 1977 in Barranquilla, Colombia. Her father is originally from the United States, born in New York, at 5 years old his family moved to Sincelejo from New York then relocated to Barranquilla. She is the only child of Nidia Ripoll and William Mebarak Chadid and is of Lebanese (Arab), Spanish (Catalan), and Italian descent. She has eight older half-siblings from her father's previous marriage.

Statue of Shakira in Barranquilla, Colombia

She spent much of her youth in Barranquilla, a city located in northern Colombia. Shakira wrote her first poem, entitled "La Rosa De Cristal" ("The Crystal Rose") when she was only four years old. As she was growing up, she was fascinated watching her father writing stories on a typewriter, and asked for one as a Christmas gift. She got her wish at age seven and continued writing poetry. These poems eventually evolved into songs. At the age of two, an older half-brother was killed in a motorcycle accident and at the age of eight, Shakira wrote her first song entitled "Tus gafas oscuras" ("Your dark glasses") which was inspired by her father, who for years wore dark glasses, to hide his grief. When Shakira was four, her father took her to a local Middle Eastern restaurant, where Shakira first heard the doumbek, a traditional drum used in Arabic music and which typically accompanied belly dancing. Before she knew it, Shakira was dancing on the table, she then knew she wanted to be a performer. She enjoyed singing for schoolmates and teachers (and even the nuns) at her Catholic school, but in the second grade was rejected for the school choir because her vibrato was too strong. The music teacher told her that she sounded "like a goat". At school, she says she had been known as "the belly dancer girl", as she would demonstrate every Friday at school a number she had learned. "That's how I discovered my passion for live performance," she says.

When she was eight, Shakira's father declared bankruptcy. While the details were sorted out, she stayed with relatives in Los Angeles. On returning to Barranquilla, she was shocked to find that much of what her parents owned had been sold; as she later said "In my childish head, this was the end of the world." To show her that things could be worse, her father took her to a local park to see orphans who lived there. The images stayed with her and she said to herself "one day I'm going to help these kids when I become a famous artist." Between the ages of ten and thirteen Shakira was invited to various events in Barranquilla and gained some recognition in the area. It was at about this time that she met local theater producer Monica Ariza, who was impressed with her and as a result tried to help her career. During a flight from Barranquilla to Bogotá, Ariza convinced Sony Colombia executive Ciro Vargas to hold an audition for Shakira in a hotel lobby. Vargas held Shakira in high regard and, returning to the Sony office, gave the cassette to a song and artist director. However, the director was not overly excited and thought Shakira was something of "a lost cause". Vargas, not daunted, was still convinced that Shakira had talent, and set up an audition in Bogotá. He arranged for Sony Colombia executives to arrive at the audition, with the idea of surprising them with Shakira's performance. She performed three songs for the executives and impressed them enough for her to be signed to record three albums.

Music career

1990–94: Career beginnings

Shakira's debut album, *Magia*, was recorded with Sony Music Columbia in 1990 when she was only thirteen years old. The songs are a collection made by her since she was 8, mixed pop-rock ballads and disco uptempo songs with electronic accompaniment, however it was hampered by a lack of recording and production cohesion. The album was released in June 1991 and featured "Magia" and three other singles. Though it fared well on Colombian radio and gave the young Shakira much exposure, the album did not fare well commercially as only 1,200 copies were sold worldwide. After the poor performance of *Magia*, Shakira's label urged her to return to the studio to release a follow-up record. Although little known outside of her native Colombia, Shakira was invited to perform at Chile's Viña del Mar International Song Festival in February 1993. The festival gave aspiring Latin American singers a chance to perform their songs, and the winner was then chosen by a panel of judges. Shakira performed the ballad "Eres" ("You Are") and won the trophy for third place. One of the judges who voted for her to win was then 20-year-old Ricky Martin.

Shakira's second studio album *Peligro* was released in March, but Shakira was not pleased with the final result, mainly taking issue with the production. The album was better received than *Ma-*

gia, though it was also considered a commercial failure due to Shakira's refusal to advertise it. Shakira then decided to take a hiatus from recording so that she could graduate from high. In the same year, Shakira starred in the Colombian TV Series "The Oasis", loosely based on the Armero tragedy in 1985. Since then, the albums have been pulled from release and are not considered official Shakira albums but rather promotional albums.

1995–97: *Pies Descalzos* and *The Remixes*

Shakira originally recorded the song "¿Dónde Estás Corazón?" (later released on her album *Pies Descalzos*) for the compilation album *Nuestro Rock* in 1995, released exclusively in Colombia. "Pies Descalzos" album brought her great popularity in Latin America by the hit singles "Estoy Aquí," "Pies Descalzos, Sueños Blancos" and "Dónde Estás Corazón." Shakira also recorded three tracks in Portuguese titled "Estou Aqui", "Um Pouco de Amor", and "Pés Descalços".

Shakira returned to recording music under Sony Music along with Columbia in 1995 with Luis F. Ochoa, using musical influences from a number of countries and an Alanis Morissette-oriented persona which affected two of her next albums. These recordings spawned her third studio album but first official, *Pies Descalzos*. Recording for the album began in February 1995, after the success of her single "¿Dónde Estás Corazón?". Sony gave Shakira $100,000 to produce the album since they predicted that the album would not sell past 100,000 copies. Starting with this album, Shakira began producing her own music, perfecting her vocals and most of all, practicing creative control over her music. Highly influenced by the American alternative market and British groups such as *The Pretenders*, the album's songs are melodic, musically surprising and gritty, with intellectual lyrics and an electronic/acoustic blend that effectively broke the formulaic mold of Latin pop with an authentic sound that had not been heard before.

The album *Pies Descalzos*, was released in October 1995 in South America and in February 1996 internationally. It debuted at number one in eight different countries. However, it only managed to reach number one-hundred-eighty on the U.S. Billboard 200 but reached number five on the U.S. Billboard Top Latin Albums chart. The album spawned six hit singles, "Estoy Aquí" which reached number two on the U.S. Latin chart, "¿Dónde Estás Corazón?" which reached number five on the U.S. Latin chart, "Pies Descalzos, Sueños Blancos" which reached number eleven on the U.S. Latin chart, "Un Poco De Amor" which reached number six on the U.S. Latin chart, "Antología" which reached number fifteen on the U.S. Latin Pop Songs chart and "Se Quiere, Se Mata" which reached number eight on the U.S. Latin chart. In August 1996, RIAA certified the album platinum status.

In March 1996, Shakira went on to her first international tour named simply the *Tour Pies Descalzos*. The tour consisted of 20 shows and ended in 1997. Also in that year, Shakira received three Billboard Latin Music Awards for Album of the Year for *Pies Descalzos*, Video of the Year for "Estoy Aqui" and Best New Artist. *Pies Descalzos* later sold over 5 million copies, prompting the release of a remix album, simply titled *The Remixes*. *The Remixes* also included Portuguese versions of some of her well known songs, which were recorded as a result of her success in the Brazilian market, where *Pies Descalzos* sold nearly one million copies.

1998–2000: *Dónde Están Los Ladrones?* and *MTV Unplugged*

Her second official studio album, *Dónde Están Los Ladrones?*, produced entirely by Shakira herself and Emilio Estefan, Jr. as the executive producer, was released in September 1998. The album, inspired by an incident in an airport in which a suitcase full of her written lyrics was stolen, became a bigger hit than *Pies Descalzos*. Allmusic and Rolling Stone both gave the album a four out of five stars rating. The album has reached a peak position of number one-hundred-thirty-one on the U.S. *Billboard 200* and held the top spot on the U.S. Latin Albums chart for eleven weeks. It has since sold over 1.5 million copies in the U.S. alone, making it one of the best selling Spanish albums in the U.S. Eight of the album's eleven tracks became singles, including "Ciega, Sordomuda", "Moscas En La Casa", "No Creo" which became her first single to chart on the U.S. *Billboard* Hot 100, "Inevitable", "Tú", "Si Te Vas", "Octavo Día", and the world-famous, Arabic tinged "Ojos Así". The latter two songs won Shakira one Latin Grammy each with six of the eight singles reaching the top 40 on the U.S. Latin chart.

Dónde Están Los Ladrones? has sold seven million copies worldwide. Shakira also received her first Grammy Award nomination in 1999 for Best Latin Rock/Alternative Album. Shakira's first live album, *MTV Unplugged* was recorded in New York City on August 12, 1999. Highly acclaimed by American critics, it is rated as one of her best-ever live performances. The live album earned the Grammy Award for Best Latin Pop Album in 2001 and gained sales of five million worldwide. In March 2000, Shakira embarked on her *Tour Anfibio*, a two-month tour of Latin America and the United States. In August 2000, she won an MTV Video Music Award in the now-defunct category of People's Choice — Favorite International Artist for "Ojos Asi". On September 9, 2000, Shakira performed "Ojos Así" at the inaugural ceremony of the Latin Grammy Awards, where she was nominated in five categories: Album of the Year and Best Pop Vocal Album for *MTV Unplugged*, Best Female Rock Vocal Performance for "Octavo Dia", Best Female Pop Vocal Performance and Best Short Form Music Video for the video for "Ojos Asi", but she won only two of the awards. Shakira's performance of "Ojos Asi" at the awards show was voted as the Greatest Latin Grammy performance of all time.

2001–04: *Laundry Service* and international success

Upon the success of *Dónde Están Los Ladrones?* and *MTV Unplugged*, Shakira began working on an English crossover album. Thanks to other successful crossover acts, most notably that of Ricky Martin, Selena and Enrique Iglesias, the crossover of Spanish artists to the English market had a great surge of popularity in mainstream music and it was the next logical step to Shakira and her label for her career. Shakira worked for over a year on new material for the album. "Whenever, Wherever" ("Suerte" in Spanish countries) was released as the first and lead single from Shakira's first English album and third studio album throughout the period of August 2001 and February 2002. The song took heavy influence from Andean music, including the charango and panpipes in its instrumentation. The track was produced by Shakira, and it was an international success by reaching number one in most countries. It was also her first success in the U.S., by reaching number six on the Hot 100.

Shakira's third studio album and first English language album *Laundry Service (Servicio De Lavanderia* in Latin America and Spain) was released on November 13, 2001. The album debuted at number three on the U.S. Billboard 200 chart selling over 200,000 records in its first week. *Laundry Service* was later certified triple platinum by the RIAA in June 2004 as well. and thus helped to establish Shakira's musical presence in the mainstream North American market. Seven songs from the album became international singles: "Whenever, Wherever" / "Suerte", "Underneath Your Clothes", "Objection (Tango)" / "Te Aviso, Te Anuncio (Tango)", "The One", "Te Dejo Madrid", "Que Me Quedes Tú" and "Poem To A Horse", with four of the singles becoming largely successful.

Because the album was created for the English language market, the rock and Spanish dance-influenced album gained mild critical success with some critics claimed that her English skills were too weak for her to write songs for it with *Rolling Stone* stating "she sounds downright silly" or "Shakira's magic is lost in translation." Shakira also was criticized by her Latin fans for seemingly abandoning her folk and rock roots in favor of contemporary American pop music. Despite this fact, the album became the best selling album of 2002, selling more than 13 million copies worldwide. and became the most successful album of her career to date. Around this time, Shakira also released four songs for Pepsi for her promotion in the English markets: "Ask for More", "Pide Mas", "Knock on My Door" and "Pideme El Sol", included in the extended play, Pepsi CD.

In November 2002, Shakira embarked on the Tour of the Mongoose with 61 shows occurring by May 2003. The tour was also her first worldwide tour, as legs were played in North and South America as well as Europe and Asia. At Aerosmith's MTV Icon in April 2002, Shakira performed "Dude (Looks Like a Lady)". Also in 2002, Shakira joined the likes of Cher, Whitney Houston, Celine Dion, Mary J. Blige, Anastacia, and the Dixie Chicks for *VH1 Divas Live Las Vegas*. In September 2002, Shakira won the now-defunct International Viewer's Choice Award at the MTV Video Music Awards with "Whenever, Wherever". Shakira also won the Latin Grammy Award for the category of Best Short Form Music Video for the Spanish version of the video. In October of that year, she won five MTV Video Music Awards Latin America for Best Female Artist, Best Pop Artist, Best Artist – North (Region), Video of the Year (for "Suerte"), and Artist of the Year. In November 2002, Shakira's label Sony BMG released her Spanish greatest hits compilation *Grandes Éxitos*. A DVD and ten-track live album, called *Live & Off the Record*, was also released in 2004, reaching sales of 3 million worldwide, and commemorating the Tour of the Mongoose.

2005–08: *Fijación Oral Vol. 1* and *Oral Fixation Vol. 2*

Shakira at the Rock in Rio festival in 2008

After promotion for Shakira's third studio album ended in 2003, Shakira chose to step out of the spotlight to record new music. Many possible release dates for her fourth studio album were announced but later delayed until early 2005 when Shakira announced the title of her fourth record and that Rick Rubin would be the executive producer of the album. It was later announced that the album would instead be two albums. Shakira's fourth studio album, *Fijación Oral Vol. 1*, was released in June 2005. The lead single from the album, "La Tortura" reached the top 40 of on the Hot 100 after being released in April 2005 and receiving large scale success on radio. The song also featured the Spanish balladeer Alejandro Sanz. It also spent a record of twenty-five weeks at number one on the U.S. Latin chart. Shakira became the first artist to perform a Spanish language song at the *MTV Video Music Awards* in 2005 as well.

Contrary to low expectations, *Fijación Oral Vol. 1* was extremely well received. It debuted at number four on the *Billboard 200* chart, selling 157,000 copies in its first week. It has since sold over two million copies in the U.S., earning a 2x Platinum certification from the RIAA. Due to its first week sales, the album became the highest debut ever for a Spanish language album. After only a day of release in Latin America, the album earned certifications. In Venezuela, it earned a Platinum certification, in Colombia, a triple Platinum certification while in Mexico, the album exceeded shipments and was unavailable after only one day of release. The album sold over one million copies in three days worldwide. Four other singles were also released from the album. "No", "Dia De Enero", "La Pared" and "Las De La Intuición", with each single reaching number one in countries worldwide.

On February 8, 2006, Shakira won her second Grammy Award with the win of *Best Latin Rock/Alternative Album* for *Fijación Oral Vol. 1*. Shakira received four Latin Grammy Awards in November 2006, winning the awards for Record of the Year, Song of the Year for "La Tortura", Album of the Year and Best Pop Vocal Album for *Fijación Oral Vol. 1*. *Fijación Oral Vol. 1* has since sold over 4 million copies worldwide.

Before the release of *Oral Fixation Vol. 2*, Shakira's second bilingual studio album, Shakira appeared at the MTV Europe Music Awards 2005 in Lisbon, Portugal, where she performed "Don't Bother", the lead single from the album, minutes before winning an award in the category of Best Female Artist. "Don't Bother", however, failed to achieve chart success in the U.S. by missing the top 40 on the Hot 100. It did, however, reach the top 20 in most countries worldwide. Shakira's second English studio album and fifth studio album, *Oral Fixation Vol. 2* was released on November 29, 2005. The album debuted at number five on the *Billboard 200*, selling 128,000 copies in its first week. The album has gone on to sell 1.8 million records in the U.S., earning a Platinum certification from the RIAA. Oddly enough, the album did not fare as well as its Spanish counterpart in the U.S., selling a few hundred thousand less records overall. *Oral Fixation Vol. 2* has also gone on to sell over 8 million copies worldwide. The cover of the album featured Shakira as Eve with forbidden fruit was also considered controversial, and had to be altered in several countries which would not sell the album with that cover.

Despite the commercial failure of the album's lead single in the U.S., it went on to spawn two more singles. "Hips Don't Lie", featuring Wyclef Jean, was released as the album's second single in February 2006. The song went on to become the highest selling single of the 21st century and became Shakira's first number one single on the Billboard Hot 100, in addition to reaching number one in over fifty-five countries. Shakira and Wyclef Jean also recorded a Bamboo version of the song to serve as the official theme of the FIFA World Cup 2006. Shakira, along with the Red Hot Chili Peppers, received the most nominations for the 2006 MTV Video Music Awards with "Hips Don't Lie", but she won only the award for Best Choreography. Shakira later released the third and final single from the album, "Illegal" featuring Carlos Santana, in November 2006. The single reached number one in some European countries and on the U.S. dance chart, though it failed to reach the Hot 100.Shakira embarked on the Oral Fixation Tour, in June 2006. The tour consisted of 125 shows between June 2006 and July 2007. The concert also visited all six continents. One show in Mexico City was performed for free, and earned an audience of over 200,000. This concert sets the record for the highest attendance of any concert in Mexican history. Shakira also performed on July 9, 2006 at the FIFA World Cup final in Germany. In November 2007, the *Oral Fixation Tour* DVD was released and is also available in High Definition Blu-Ray format. The two versions of the DVD have sold over 16 million copies worldwide. In February 2007, Shakira performed for the first time at the 49th Grammy Awards and earned the nomination for Best Pop Collaboration with Vocals for "Hips Don't Lie" with Wyclef Jean, though she did not win the award.

2009–present: *She Wolf* and *Sale el Sol*

During an online chat with her fans in *El Heraldo* in February 2008, Shakira revealed that work on her sixth studio album was about to begin. Furthermore, at Shakira's cousin Isa Mebarak's album release party in Colombia, Shakira's father William Mebarak stated that Shakira was currently at work writing and producing new songs for her upcoming album. This was being done in "her own studio", which many fans thought to mean the studio at her home in the Bahamas. Shakira recorded 2005's *Fijación Oral Vol. 1* and 2006's *Oral Fixation Vol. 2* there as well.

After spending two weeks in London, Shakira flew to Colombia for a peace-promoting concert in Leticia (at the three way border of Colombia, Peru and Brazil) with Carlos Vives. Followed by hundreds of thousands of fellow Colombians, Shakira was calling for the release of hostages being held by rebels in Colombia and an end to similar kidnappings in the region. Afterward, it was reported by Noticias Caracol in Colombia that Shakira returned to her home studio in the Bahamas and continued recording "a little something" with members of Vives' band. It was later confirmed that Shakira was working with the likes of RedOne, Wyclef Jean and Luis F. Ochoa on her sixth studio album. RedOne later stated that Shakira was in "an experimental phase" and that she had been working on the album in Los Angeles, Miami, Vancouver, London, Uruguay and the Bahamas.

In early 2008, Forbes named Shakira the fourth top-earning female artist in music industry. Then, in July 2008, Shakira signed a 10-year contract with Live Nation, an international touring giant. The touring group also doubles as a record label which promotes but does control the music their artists release. Regarding Shakira's contract, Jason Garner, the global music chief of Live Nation stated that: "Shakira is one of the few truly global artists. She can sell music and tickets in nearly every corner of the globe." Neither Shakira's representatives nor Live Nation would confirm the value of the deal, but people close to the negotiations said that depending on Shakira's performance over the 10 years, it is likely to be worth between $70 million and $100 million. Shakira's contract with Epic Records calls for three more albums as well – one in English, one in Spanish, and a compilation, but the touring and other rights of the Live Nation deal were confirmed to begin immediately.

Shakira at the 2010 NBA All-Star Game

"She Wolf", the lead single from Shakira's sixth studio album, premiered on July 13, 2009. Shakira wrote and produced the song with John Hill, and Sam Endicott (lead singer and songwriter of The Bravery). The Spanish version, titled "Loba", premiered on the same day as well. "She Wolf" and "Loba" then became available for digital download the following day. The video for "She Wolf" premiered on MTV on July 30, 2009. The single was successful worldwide, reaching number one in Latin America, number two in Germany, Ireland, Italy, Estonia and Spain, number three in Switzerland and Austria, number four in the UK, France and Greece, number five in Canada and Belgium, number six in Finland, number nine in Japan, and number eleven in the US.

Also in July 2009, Shakira's official website announced that "The full album is *She Wolf* due out in October 2009 from Epic" and it "features a predominantly English track list". The site also announced that a Spanish album will be released in 2010. *She Wolf* was released in October 2009 internationally and on November 23, 2009 in the U.S.

The album received mainly positive reviews from critics, but only managed to sell 89,000 copies in its first week in the U.S., earning the number fifteen spot on the Billboard 200. It has gone on to sell only 300,000 records in the U.S., becoming her least successful album there. However, the album has been moderately successful worldwide, having been certified Gold in Russia, Ireland, Switzerland, Poland, France, Argentina, Greece, and Hungary, Platinum in Spain, the United Kingdom, and the Middle East, 2x Platinum in Colombia and Mexico, and 3x Platinum in Taiwan. To date the album has sold 1.5 million copies worldwide, becoming Shakira's least successful studio album to date in terms of sales.

The album's second single, "Did It Again", was released in October 2009 and was originally due for a U.S. release, though this was later canceled. The single reached the top 40 in most countries worldwide. "Give It Up To Me", featuring Lil Wayne was released as the album's second U.S. single in November 2009 and reached the top 40 in Canada and on the Hot 100. The album's U.S. release was delayed in order for Shakira to record the song, which was originally due to be featured on its producer Timbaland's album, *Timbaland Presents Shock Value II* and would have featured Shakira. However, she chose to record it for her album with Timbaland's rap verse being scrapped in favor of a verse from Flo Rida. Plans for the single changed again when Lil Wayne requested to be featured on the song, with this later happening. The album's third and final single, "Gypsy", was released in February 2010 and reached the top 40 in Europe but failed to reach the top 40 in the U.S. or in South America, becoming a mildly successful single. In May 2010, it was confirmed through Shakira's official website that she will embark on a global tour. The site announced that the tour will begin in North America in September 2010. The post also announced the first three confirmed dates and stated that additional dates will be announced soon, adding that "The tour will bring Shakira's spectacular show to top arenas and a host of additional cities throughout the summer and fall".

It was initially announced that Shakira would release a Spanish album in 2010 after the release of *She Wolf*, similar to what she did with *Oral Fixation*, but Shakira later stated that the album would instead be a bilingual project, which will contain Spanish and English songs. She also stated that it was due for a September 2010 release. Shakira collaborated with the South African group Freshlyground to create the official song of the 2010 FIFA World Cup in South Africa. "Waka Waka (This Time for Africa)", which is based on a traditional Cameroonian soldiers' Fang song named "Zangalewa" by the group Zangalewa or Golden Sounds. The song was made popular in her native Colombia in 1987 through west African DJs in Colombia. The single later reached the top 20 in Europe, South America and Africa and the top 40 in the U.S. and was performed by Shakira at the World Cup kick-off and closing.

Sale el Sol has been released as Shakira's seventh studio album on October 19, 2010. In June 2010, during an interview with *Billboard* magazine, Shakira announced that her new album would be released in September. She stated in the magazine that "I see it [the new album] as having two currents," she stated. "One is a lot about love and love experiences and emotions. And the other side of it is very joyful, and upbeat." Shakira also revealed that the music on the album would reflect influences from both the Dominican Republic and Colombia. "It's a little more Latin on one side and a little more rock 'n roll on the other side," she stated. She later compared her new material to the *Oral Fixation* era's music, stating that she was "going back to basics" for the record. The lead single "Loca", her version of the song "Loca con su tiguere" from El Cata, was number one in many countries. She shot the video for "Loca" in Barcelona in August,. Shakira unveiled the official album cover on September 1. The album debuted at 7 on

Billboard 200 in its first week, and at the top spot on the Billboard Top Latin Albums. On December 6, 2010 Sony Music announced that the album had sold over 1 million copies worldwide in 6 weeks, and over 4 million since its release.

Shakira is currently on her The Sun Comes Out World Tour in support of her two most recent albums.

Collaborations and other work

Shakira performing with Usher and Stevie Wonder at the We Are One: The Obama Inaugural Celebration at the Lincoln Memorial.

In 2003, Shakira wrote a song called "Come Down Love" with Tim Mitchell for the Hollywood movie *The Italian Job* starring South African actress Charlize Theron and Mark Wahlberg, but the song was not included on the soundtrack of the same name. In late 2006, Shakira and Alejandro Sanz collaborated for the duet *Te lo Agradezco, Pero No*, which is featured on Sanz' album *El Tren de los Momentos*. The song was a top ten hit in Latin America, and topped "Billboard" Hot Latin Tracks chart. Shakira also collaborated with Miguel Bosé on the duet "Si Tú No Vuelves", which was released in Bosé's album *Papito*, which celebrates his thirty-year career. In early 2007, Shakira worked with American R&B singer Beyoncé for the track "Beautiful Liar", which was released as the second single from the deluxe edition of Knowles' *B'Day*. In April 2007, the single jumped ninety-one positions, from ninety-four to three, on the *Billboard* Hot 100 chart, setting the record for the largest upward movement in the history of the chart at the time. It was also number one on the official UK Singles Chart. The song earned them a Grammy Award nomination for Best Pop Collaboration with Vocals. The song was one of Knowles' most successful worldwide, as it was particularly popular in Spanish-speaking countries such as Argentina and Spain, where it topped charts.

According to *Billboard*, Shakira, along with Lil Wayne would collaborate on a new track for Carlos Santana's greatest hits CD titled *Ultimate Santana*. However, this collaboration was cancelled, and Shakira and Lil Wayne were replaced by Jennifer Lopez and Baby Bash. Shakira is featured on Annie Lennox's song "Sing", from the album *Songs of Mass Destruction*, which also features other twenty-three other female singers such as Madonna, KT Tunstall, Faith Hill, Dido, Celine Dion, Melissa Etheridge, Joss Stone, Fergie, Anastacia and Pink. In late 2007, Shakira and Wyclef Jean recorded their second duet "King and Queen". The song was featured on Wyclef Jean's 2007 album *Carnival Vol. II: Memoirs of an Immigrant*.

Shakira in January 2009

Shakira performed on January 18, 2009 at the Lincoln Memorial "We Are One" festivities in honor of the inauguration of President Barack Obama. She performed "Higher Ground" with Stevie Wonder and Usher. She also performed during the evening of January 20, 2009 at the Neighborhood Ball for the President's inauguration. The song she performed was Van Morrison's "Bright Side of the Road". It featured Shakira on harmonica. In March 2009, Shakira appeared on the album *Cantora 1* by the Argentinian folk singer Mercedes Sosa on the song "La Maza", which both singers sang at the ALAS concert in Buenos Aires in May 2008. Shakira wrote the lyrics and co-wrote the music for two new songs that are featured in the movie *Love in the Time of Cholera*, based on the acclaimed novel by Colombian author Gabriel García Marquez. García Marquez himself asked Shakira to write the songs. The songs that Shakira lent to the soundtrack were "Pienso en ti", a song from Shakira's breakthrough album *Pies Descalzos*, "Hay Amores" and "Despedida". "Despedida" was nominated for Best Original Song at the 65th Golden Globe Awards but did not win. It was rumored that the song would also be nominated for an Academy Award, but it was not, with a source calling the fact that it was left off the nominees the Academy's "worst snub.

Shakira collaborated with the South African group Freshlyground to create the official song of the 2010 FIFA World Cup in South Africa, "Waka Waka (This Time for Africa)". She headlined the closing ceremony on July 11, 2010 as well.

In August of 2010, Shakira recorded a song with Dora the Explorer called "Todos Juntos." The song is featured on the soundtrack *We Did It! Dora's Greatest Hits*, which was released on August 17, 2010. The song was also featured on a Dora television special titled "Dora's Explorer Girls" which aired on November 7, 2010 on Nickelodeon.

Other work

Shakira appeared in the Colombian telenovela *El Oasis* in 1994, playing the character of Luisa Maria. In December 2009, Shakira appeared as herself in the *Ugly Betty* episode "The Bahamas Triangle". In 2010, Shakira appeared as a fictional version herself in an episode of *Wizards of Waverly Place*. She was also mentioned several times on The George

Lopez Show. She was invited personally by Gabriel Garcia Marquez to play a role in *Love in the Time of Cholera*, but declined due to the nudity involved.

Shakira is well known for her dancing in various music videos and in concert. Her moves are based on the art of belly dancing, a part of her Lebanese heritage. She often performs barefoot. Shakira says she learned this form of dance as a young teen to overcome her shyness. She also mentioned in a MTV interview that she learned how to belly dance by trying to flip a coin with her belly. The intense training has afforded her a fluidity in her body movement most seen in the videos to her hits "Ojos Así", "La Tortura", "Hips Don't Lie", "Whenever, Wherever / Suerte", "Beautiful Liar" "and "She Wolf / Loba". She has had several belly dance choreographers, including award-winning Bellydance Superstar Boženka. As the MTV *Making the Video* for "La Tortura" reveals, she worked with Jamie King on the choreography, but ended up creating most of it herself.

Shakira became the 2010 celebrity spokesperson for the Freixenet traditional Christmas TV commercial. Each year, this Cava company taps into a world-famous celebrity to be the face of its much-awaited holiday TV spot. For her latest venture, Shakira dressed up as a golden sparkling wine bubble, "This year, let's toast so that the sun shines more than ever. The best is yet to come. Merry Christmas." Shakira says in the ad. In a press conference in Barcelona, Shakira presented the Christmas commercial, which will start airing in Spain on December 9. The singer also took the opportunity to announce that she used the $500,000 EUR ($662,085 USD) honorarium given to her by the Spanish bubbly to finance two schools run by her foundation, Pies Descalzos. The partnership between Shakira and Freixenet also includes a Pies Descalzos Foundation promotional video, directed by longtime Shakira collaborator and fellow Catalan Jaume Delaiguana.

Philanthropy

In 1995, Shakira founded the Pies Descalzos Foundation. It is a Colombian charity with special schools for poor children all around Colombia. It was funded by Shakira and other international groups and individuals. The name of the foundation is taken from Shakira's third studio album called *Pies Descalzos*, released in 1995. During her career, Shakira has performed at a large number of benefit concerts. In 2002 she sang at a Party in the Park concert fundraising for the Prince's Trust. That same year she performed at Divas Live which supports VH1's Save the Music Foundation. On July 2, 2005, she performed her hits "Whenever, Wherever" and "La Tortura" on the Live 8 benefit concert at the Palace of Versailles, near Paris. On July 7, 2007, the singer opened the German leg of Live Earth in Hamburg. Her set included "Don't Bother", "Inevitable", "Día Especial" (with Gustavo Cerati) and "Hips Don't Lie". Shakira also performed at the "Clinton Global Initiative", where she performed her hits "Underneath Your Clothes", "Inevitable" and "Hips Don't Lie". On May 17, 2008 Shakira and twenty other Latin American and Spanish artists performed in Buenos Aires and Mexico City to raise money for Shakira's Latin America in Solidarity Action "America Latina en Accion Solidaria" (ALAS Foundation) charity. This concert attracted 150,000 people in Buenos Aires. Although tickets were free, the demand exceeded the supply; some fans who were fortunate enough to secure free tickets resold them.

Shakira, Alejandro Sanz and the King of Spain during the IberoAmerican Summit of El Salvador

She has agitated against the implementation of the Arizona statute SB1070 against illegal immigration, saying that it goes against civil rights.

Shakira is a UNICEF Goodwill Ambassador and is one of their global representatives. "Shakira, like all our Goodwill Ambassadors, was chosen based on her compassion, her involvement in global issues, her deep commitment to helping children, and her appeal to young people around the world. We're very pleased to have Shakira join the UNICEF family. I know she'll help bring UNICEF's mission to the audience who will have the most impact on our future – young people themselves", said UNICEF's Executive Director Carol Bellamy.

On April 3, 2006, Shakira was honored at a UN ceremony for creating the Pies Descalzos Foundation. At the event, the singer said, "Let's not forget that at the end of this day when we all go home, 960 children will have died in Latin America." On September 28, 2007 at the Clinton Global Initiative, it was revealed that Shakira received a commitment of $40 million from the Spanish government to help the victims of natural disasters. An additional $5 million was to be donated to four Latin American countries, to be spent on education and health. As part of the May 2007 concerts, her ALAS Foundation was able to solicit commitments of US$ 200 million from philanthropists Carlos Slim, Mexico's richest man, and Howard Buffett, son of U.S. investment guru Warren Buffett, the singer announced on April 15, 2008. In December 2007, Shakira visited Bangladesh to appeal for the victims of Cyclone Sidr. She spent 3 days with the victims and visited children affected by the disaster in schools built by UNICEF and participated in the distribution of family kits and warm clothes. She said that little was left of the school she visited in the village of Mirzapur, but it still provided an "oasis" for the children. "I am more convinced than ever that education is the key to so many of the difficulties that our children face in countries like mine or in developing countries like this one. It's the key to a better and safer world," she said.

Shakira served as the Honorary Chairperson for "Action Week" 2008 (April 21–27). The event is sponsored by the Global Campaign for Education (GCE), to generate awareness about the Education for All Act. She spoke with the U.S. Congress, British Prime Minister Gordon Brown, and World Bank President Robert Zoellick to promote a move towards Global Education. Angelina Jolie served as last year's chair. People En Español announced in their December 2008/January 2009 issue that Shakira is the "Humanitarian of the Year" as part of their "Las Estrellas del Año" (Stars of the Year) awards. Shakira was also ranked at number 48 on the list of Top 50 Most Charitable Celebrities by OK! magazine. It reported that she donates approximately $55,000 to charity yearly. On her 32nd birthday, Shakira opened a new $6-Million school in her hometown Barranquilla, which was sponsored by herself and her Pies Descalzos Foundation.

On December 7, 2009 Shakira was honored as a guest at the University of Oxford to give a speech about her work with children and education. She was chosen by the Oxford Union and joined the ranks of Albert Einstein, several US Presidents, Mother Teresa, and the Dalai Lama XIV, as a chosen speaker. During the speech, Shakira said, "That is how I want the youth of 2060 to see us: That our mission for global peace consisted of sending 30,000 educators to Afghanistan, not 30,000 soldiers. That in 2010, world education became more important than world domination."

In March 2010, she was awarded a medal by the UN' International Labor Organization in recognition of being, as UN Labor Chief Juan Somavia put it, a "true ambassador for children and young people, for quality education and social justice." In November 2010, after performing as the opening act of the MTV European Music Awards, the Colombian singer also received the MTV Free Your Mind award for her continuing dedication to improve access to education for all children around the world.

In February 2011, the FC Barcelona Foundation and *Pies descalzos* reached an agreement for children's education through sport.

Personal life

Relationships

In 2000, Shakira started dating Antonio de la Rúa. In a 2009 interview, Shakira stated their relationship already worked as a married couple, and that "they don't need papers for that." On January 10, 2011, Shakira announced on her website that after 11 years together, she and de la Rúa had separated in August 2010 after making "a mutual decision to take time apart from our romantic relationship." She wrote that the couple "view this period of separation as temporary and as a time of individual growth as we continue to be partners in our business and professional lives", with de la Rúa overseeing Shakira's "business and career interests as he has always done."

Shakira has currently been dating Gerard Piqué (10 years younger centre back for FC Barcelona). Shakira officially confirmed their relationship on March 29, 2011 via Twitter and Facebook posting a picture of the two with a caption reading, "I present to you my sunshine." It was the first time she'd ever spoken of the relationship.

Other

Shakira was raised as a Roman Catholic. She met personally the pope John Paul II in 1998, who nominated her a Goodwill Ambassador. She is interested in world history and frequently studies the history and languages of the countries she visits. After her Oral Fixation tour ended in summer 2007, Shakira attended a class in Los Angeles at UCLA, on the History of Western Civilization. She used her middle and last names, Isabel Mebarak, and told the professor she was visiting from Colombia so as to avoid being recognized as a celebrity. Shakira is a cousin of model and 2005–2006 Miss Colombia, Valerie Domínguez.

Style

Music and voice

Shakira is known to have adopted many genres, including folk, mainstream pop and rock. In an interview with *Rolling Stone* she said: "My music, I think, is a fusion of many different elements. And I'm always experimenting. So I try not to limit myself, or put myself in a category, or... be the architect of my own jail". Her earlier Spanish albums, including *Pies Descalzos* and *¿Dónde Están Los Ladrones?* were a mix of folk music and Latin rock, while her crossover English album, *Laundry Service* and her later albums were influenced by pop rock and pop Latino. Her 2009 album, *She Wolf* is more like electropop and dance music. Her 2010 album, *Sale el Sol*, is a return to her beginnings containing ballads such as "Lo Que Más" and "Antes de las Seis", rock songs like "Tu Boca" and "Devoción", and Latin dance songs like "Loca".

Influences

Shakira has told many interviewers that she has grown fond of listening to oriental music, which influenced many of her earlier works. For example, Shakira used the Indian theme for her performance of "Hips Don't Lie" at the 2006 MTV Video Music Awards in New York City. She has also been influenced by her Arab heritage, which was a major inspiration for her breakthrough world hit "Ojos Así". She told Portuguese TV "Many of my movements belong to Arab culture." She also cites her parents as major contributors to her musical style.

In childhood, Shakira preferred rock and roll music, listening heavily to her favorite rock bands like Led Zeppelin, The Beatles, Nirvana, The Police and U2. She lists John Lennon as her No.1 musical influence. She was also deeply influenced by The Rolling Stones, AC/DC, The Who, The Pretenders, Red Hot Chili Peppers, The Cure, Tom Petty, Depeche Mode, The Clash, Ramones, whose influence can be heard on her many prominent songs. In a recent interview to *Elenco* magazine, she noted that in her opinion the perfect songs are

"Imagine" by John Lennon and "No Woman, No Cry" by Bob Marley.

Shakira made several covers of prominent artists such AC/DC and Aerosmith, using them to sing in her tours, resulting in performances of "Back in Black" and "Dude (Looks Like a Lady)" during her *Tour of the Mongoose*. She also sang the classic Elvis Presley song "Always On My Mind" at the *VH1 Divas Live*. In her 2010–2011 tour called The Sun Comes Out World Tour, she sings "Nothing Else Matters" by the heavy metal band Metallica in an oriental style. She is also strongly influenced by Andean music and South American folk music, using her native instrumentation for the Latin dance-pop "Whenever, Wherever" and "Despedida". Shakira recently performed two songs for two separate Haiti benefit events: "I'll Stand By You", by The Pretenders, and "Sólo le pido a Dios" by León Gieco.

In terms of Spanish language rock Shakira is indebited to the Argentine rock power trio Soda Stereo and to the Mexican American band Santana.

> " I have been a Cerati fan all my life when he was part of Soda Stereo and before knowing him I had already gone to three of his concerts. Both Gustavo [Cerati] and Santana has enriched me, they are my small wonders. "
>
> —Shakira

- According to Sony, Shakira is the highest-selling Colombian artist of all time, having sold more than 50 million albums worldwide.
- According to Nielsen Broadcast Data Systems, "Hips Don't Lie" was the most-played pop song in a single week in American radio history. It was played 9,637 times in one week.
- Shakira became the first artist in the history of the Billboard charts to earn the coveted number one spots on both the Top 40 Mainstream and Latin Chart in the same week doing so with "Hips Don't Lie".
- "La Tortura" broke the record on the Billboard's Hot Latin Tracks chart, appearing at No.1 more than any other single (a total of 25 non-consecutive weeks).
- According to Yahoo!, "Hips Don't Lie" is the Best-Selling Single of the Last 10 Years.
- According to Forbes Magazine, Shakira was the fourth highest-earning woman in music for 2008 behind Madonna, Barbra Streisand and Celine Dion.
- According to Nokia, Shakira has topped more music downloads in the last year than any other Latino artist has in five, and *She Wolf* topped the Top 10 Latino downloads.
- Additionally, she is the only artist from South America to reach the number-one spot on the U.S. Billboard Hot 100, the Australian ARIA chart, and the UK Singles Chart.
- Shakira was to be given a star on the Hollywood Walk of Fame in 2009, but turned the offer down citing that she did not want to be considered a star of Hollywood.
- In 2010, Shakira was ranked number five on the 'Online Video's Most Viral Artists of 2010' with 404,118,932 views.
- Shakira has become a Youtube sensation having surpassed 1 billion views on the website with Waka Waka accounting for over 250,000,000 views this year alone. She is the third person ever to have done this, after Lady Gaga and Justin Bieber.

Discography

- *Pies Descalzos* (1996)
- *Dónde Están los Ladrones?* (1998)
- *Laundry Service* (2001)
- *Fijación Oral Vol. 1* (2005)
- *Oral Fixation Vol. 2* (2005)
- *She Wolf* (2009)
- *Sale el Sol* (2010)

Tours

- 1996–1997: *Tour Pies Descalzos*
- 2000: *Tour Anfibio*
- 2002–2003: *Tour of the Mongoose*
- 2006–2007: *Oral Fixation Tour*
- 2010–2011: *The Sun Comes Out World Tour*

Source (edited): "http://en.wikipedia.org/wiki/Shakira"

Taheyya Kariokka

Tahiya Karioka (Arabic: تحية كاريوكا) also **Tahiya Mohamed** (born as: **Badaweya Mohamed Kareem Al Nirani**), (1920–September 20, 1999) was an Egyptian belly dancer and film actress. Born in the Egyptian town of Ismaileya in 1920 to Mohamed Kareem, Tahiya was discouraged from performing as a dancer by her family. Due to family differences that could not be settled with her father and brothers, she moved to Cairo to stay with an old neighbour, Suad Mahasen, a night club owner and an artist. Tahiya had asked several times for employment in Suad's nightclub but Suad refused to employ her due to the disreputability of working at a night club. However, many of Suad's associates and friends became acquainted with Tahiya through various visits to Suad's home. They all advised Suad to add her to one of the shows as a chorus girl but still she refused. Soon, Tahiya was mentioned to Badia Masabni, the owner of Casino Opera, one of the most prominent nightclubs of the time. Badia offered a position in her troupe to Tahiya. Tahiya accepted and was given the stage name Tahiya Mohamed. She soon began gaining popularity as a solo dancer and as she became more experienced she learned a popular Samba dance from Brasil at the time called the Karioka. After that she became known as Tahiya Karioca. Tahiya began starring in movies during what is dubbed as the Egyptian film industries "Golden Age". She was a talented dancer, singer, and actor.

Tahiya was married 14 times; among her husbands were actor Rushdy Abaza and playwright Fayez Halawa. Tahiya was unable to conceive any children of her own and hence aopted a daughter (Atiyat Allah). Tahiya also was very involved with her sibling's children. Tahiya later moved to London.

Filmography

- *Marcides (Film, 1993)*
- *Iskanderija, kaman oue kaman... aka Alexandria Again and Forever (Film, 1990)*
- *Adieu Bonaparte... aka Weda'an Bonapart (Film, 1985)*
- *Saqqa mat, al-... aka The Water-Carrier Is Dead (Film, 1977)*
- *Tareek, al-... aka The Road (Film, 1964)*
- *Hira wa chebab... aka * Ana zanbi eh?... aka Is It My Fault? (Film, 1953)*
- *Ibn al ajar... aka A Child for Rent (Film, 1953)*
- *Muntasir, El... aka The Conqueror (Film, 1952)*
- *Omm el katila, El... aka The Criminal Mother (Film, 1952)*
- *Zuhur el fatina, El... aka Charming Flowers (Film, 1952)*
- *Ibn el halal... aka The True-born Son (Film, 1951)*
- *Khadaini abi... aka My Father Deceived Me (Film, 1951)*
- *Akbal el bakari... aka A Large Family (Film, 1950)*
- *Ayni bi-triff... aka My Eye Is Winking (Film, 1950)*
- *Aheb el raks... aka I Like Dancing (Film, 1949)*
- *Amirat el djezira... aka The Princess of the Island (Film, 1949)*
- *Katel, El... aka The Murderer (Film, 1949)*
- *Mandeel al helu... aka The Beauty's Veil (Film, 1949)*
- *Hub wa junun... aka Love and Madness (Film, 1948)*
- *Ibn el fellah... aka The Peasant's Son (Film, 1948)*
- *Yahia el fann... aka Long Live Art (Film, 1948)*
- *Li'bat al sitt... aka The Lady's Puppet (Film, 1946)*
- *Ma akdarshi... aka I Can't Do It (Film, 1946)*
- *Najaf (Film, 1946)*
- *Sabr tayeb, El... aka Have Patience (Film, 1946)*
- *Aheb el baladi... aka I Like Home Cooking (Film, 1945)*
- *Hub El awal, El... aka First Love (Film, 1945)*
- *Lailat el jumaa... aka Friday Evening (Film, 1945)*
- *Naduga (Film, 1944)*
- *Rabiha-takiet el ekhfaa... aka The Magic Hat (Film, 1944)*
- *Taqiyyat al ikhfa (Film, 1944)*
- *Ahlam El chabab... aka Dreams of Youth (Film, 1943)*
- *Ahib Al ghalat... aka I Like Mistakes (Film, 1942)*

Source (edited): "http://en.wikipedia.org/wiki/Taheyya_Kariokka"

Terezka Drnzik

Terezka Drnzik is one of the matriarch figures in the Australian bellydancing community, having started the first dedicated bellydance studio in Sydney in 1989. The school has produced many professional dancers including Jrisi Jusakos of Hathor Dance and Kaeshi Chai of Bellydance Superstars.

Of Czechoslovakian/New Zealand descent, Terezka was introduced to bellydancing when she arrived in Australia in 1979 and saw Rozeta Ahalyea performing in a Greek nightclub. Terezka approached Rozetta who took her under her wing.

In 1980 Terezka lived in a household with three Arabic families, absorbing their tradition and culture. She was influenced by the stars of the 1930s to the 1950s and considers Soheir Zaki, who was prominent in the 1970s, as her greatest teacher — even though they never met.

Turning professional in 1981 Terezka was given the Arabic name of "Leila" (Night). She regularly performed seven shows per night and quickly established herself as one of three top performers in Sydney. This was a time when Arabic food, clubs and restaurants were in their heyday, with the influx of Arabs to Australia due to the Lebanese Civil War.

In 1982 Terezka performed with the renowned Egyptian Baladi singer Ahmed Adaweyah and the famed composer and piano accordion player Hussan Abou Seoud and his orchestra from Paris. As a result, she was offered a contract in Paris, where she performed six nights a week at Vildizler, La Lampe d'Aladin and Al Badiya as well as at numerous functions for the upper echelons of Paris. Contracts followed in London (at the Omar Khyaam performing alongside Mona Sayeed) as well as Belgium, Spain, and Morocco and Tunisia.

Terezka returned to Australia to open Sydney's first full-time Middle Eastern dance studio. Her mission was to present Arabic dance in an intelligent and sensitive way, staying true to the cultural aspects.

Terezka aimed to present the dance form to the Arabic community in a way that hadn't been seen before, incorporating traditional group dances as well as cabaret and contemporary in full theatrical performance. Her shows included group dances presenting contemporary (Pharaonic) pieces, traditional Beledi, Saidi and Khaleegy and stunning soloists with an emphasis on Arabic interpretation, technique and spirit in movement and performance skills.

Terezka's Academy of Danse Orientale is now one of the pre-eminent schools in Sydney. One of her innovations is classes and workshops accompanied by live musicians, a rare opportunity for dancers at intermediate and advanced levels to experience live musical accompaniment.

In 1991 Terezka hosted an evening with live musicians for the first Bellydance-a-thon, an event that turned into the annual Sydney Middle Eastern Dance Festival.

In 1992 Terezka retired from performance on the Arabic nightclub and restaurant circuit.

In 2006 Terezka was Australia's representative teacher at the Cairo Dance Festival.

Terezka has now set up a charity call Make a Child Smile, which sponsors children from developing nations. The charity's main fundraising events are gala bellydancing balls.

Source (edited): "http://en.wikipedia.org/wiki/Terezka_Drnzik"

Zeinat Olwi

Zeinat Olwi (Arabic: زينات علوي) whose stage name was **Zurah**, (1930-1988) was one of the leading belly dancers in Egypt in the middle of the twentieth century. She appeared in many movies from the Egyptian Golden Age of cinema. One of her most famous performances was in Henry Barakat's 1955 movie *Ayyam wa layali (Days and Nights)*.

Anglicizations of her name

Her given name is anglicized variously as Zeinat, Zinat, Zinaat, and Zenat. Her surname is variously given as Olwi, Elwi, Aloui.

- *Ayyam wa layali (Days and Nights)* (1955)
- video clips for Zeinat Olwi in Egyptian movies

Source (edited): "http://en.wikipedia.org/wiki/Zeinat_Olwi"

American Bellydancer

American Bellydancer is a 2005 documentary film directed by Jonathan Brandeis. It features Bellydancers including Ansuya, Rachel Galoob-Ortega, Suhaila Salimpour, Rachel Brice and Sonia.

Source (edited): "http://en.wikipedia.org/wiki/American_Bellydancer"

American Tribal Style Belly Dance

Tribal-style belly dancers in Pacifica, California (2004).

American Tribal Style Belly Dance or **Tribal Style Belly Dance** (also known as **ATS** or **Tribal**) is a modern style of bellydance created by FatChanceBellyDance director, Carolena Nericcio. American Tribal Style Belly Dance is clearly defined and documented with the primary characteristic being that of group improvisation. Tribal is generally performed in a group, often at community events such as festivals and parades, with tribal dancers typically favoring a look provided by wide-legged pants gathered at the ankles (aka pantaloons) and full skirts.

There are several American Tribal Style Belly Dance troupes in the United States. FatChanceBellyDance is one of the largest ATS dance troupe companies, providing lessons, videos, music, costumes and more. The company was formed in 1987 by Carolena Nericcio. Their website provides another perspective on the history of American Tribal Style.

Tribal style

The general category Tribal Style is accredited to Jamila Salimpour who fostered a fusion of costumes and folkloric dances styles from the Banjara gypsies of Rajasthan and began teaching what she knew and performing all over California and the West Coast. Using traditional folkloric dance elements and costumes inspired by traditional and ethnographic traditions, she presented on stage through Bal Anat a colorful dance company which included musicians, singers and dancers to create a "souk" or almost circus feel. Taking what she herself had learned from native dancers from Morocco, Algeria, Turkey, Egypt, Syria and Lebanon who were dancing in the United States, she began to catalogue "belly dance movement" and began creating a basic repertoire terminology which is still the basis for Tribal Style and American Tribal Style repertoire.

Tribal Style today represents everything from Folkloric inspired dances to a fusion of ancient dance techniques from North India, the Middle East and Africa. As a general category, Tribal Style covers many flavors of American Belly Dance both the folkloric inspired like Dalia Carella and fusion and cross over styles which explore modern, jazz, dance theatre, and hip hop with belly dance, as well as fusion with traditional classical ethnic dance forms like Bhangra, Bharata Natyam, Flamenco and now even Polynesian and West African Dance.

Tribal Style dancers (like Raqs Sharqi dancers) often use finger cymbals or zills, but the focus is on the group as opposed to emphasizing solo performance. Tribal Style does feature solos within the group as well as call-and-answer performance with another dancer (duets), or as a whole group. Often there is a chorus which provides a "drone" in the background while the featured pod is the focal point. Both the pod and the chorus are improvised in the moment. Staging for the pod and the chorus is also formalized within the ATS form to maximize dancer visibility on behalf of the audience and likewise maximizing group visibility of the leader.

Tribal style dance is characterized by muscle isolation to create smooth, undulating movements. Popular conceptions of bellydance as a seductive art have allured observers but prevented the dance form from being recognized as a legitimate art form.

According to Moria Chappell, a well-known Tribal dancer, Tribal differs from ballet, jazz and modern in its extreme emphasis of core muscle isolation (especially in the abdomen, pelvic girdle, and thoracic spine) and lack of hard impact moves. Because of the greater emphasis on muscular isolation than skeletal virtuosity, Tribal dance is accessible to people with a wider range of body types, ages, and health problems than many classic theater dance arts.

Costuming

The style is also characterized by costumes derived from many "folkloric" and various traditional tribal costuming resources and is often composed of layers of large tiered skirts or 10–25 meter/yard skirts, a short choli often with a plunging neckline, over which a bra decorated with coins and textiles sits, a headdress or hair decorations, one or more hip scarves with yarn, tassels or fringe, and a heavy layering of oxidized silver jewelry. The jewelry commonly originates from Central Asia, from any number of nomadic tribes or empires (e.g., Kuchi, Turkoman, Rajasthan) and is often large and set with semi-precious stones or, when mass-produced, with glass. Dancers frequently "tattoo" their faces with kohl or kajal. Make-up is usually eye focused with heavy use of kajal.

I can only speak for my troupe in terms of the evolution of costuming style. My teacher, Masha, encouraged us to wear a choli and pantaloons, a fringe shawl, lots of big chunky jewelry and a headdress or some sort of embellished hair worn up. The coin bra was optional. When FCBD first started we used that format, but the dancers started finding other pieces, like the full skirts and tassel belts. It was a bit of a mish-mash at first, but we eventually standardized our look to be choli, bra, pantaloons, skirt, shawl and/or tassel belt, headdress mandatory and of course lots of jewelry.

"American Tribal Style Make Up And Costuming," an interview with Carolena Nericcio by Sheri Waldrop Source (edited): "http://en.wikipedia.org/wiki/American_Tribal_Style_Belly_Dance"

Belly dance

Raqs Sharqi dancer Chryssanthi Sahar Scharf, Heidelberg.

A belly dancer in Marrakech (Morocco)

Belly dance or Bellydance is a "Western"-coined name for a traditional "Middle Eastern" dance, especially **raqs sharqi** (Arabic: رقص شرقي). It is sometimes also called **Middle Eastern dance** or **Arabic dance** in the West, or by the Greco-Turkish term **çiftetelli** (Greek: τσιφτετέλι).

The term "Belly dance" is a translation of the French "danse du ventre" which was applied to the dance in the Victorian era. It is something of a misnomer as every part of the body is involved in the dance; the most featured body part usually is the hips. Belly dance takes many different forms depending on country and region, both in costume and dance style, and new styles have evolved in the West as its popularity has spread globally. Although contemporary forms of the dance have generally been performed by women, some of the dances, particularly the cane dance, have origins in male forms of performance.

- **Raqs sharqi** (Arabic: رقص شرقي; literally "oriental dance") is the style more familiar to Westerners, performed in restaurants and

cabarets around the world. It is more commonly performed by female dancers but is also sometimes danced by men. It is a solo improvisational dance, although students often perform choreographed dances in a group.
- **Raqs baladi**, (Arabic: رقص بلدي literally "dance of country", or "folk" dance) is the folkloric style, danced socially by men and women of all ages in some Middle Eastern countries, usually at festive occasions such as weddings.

Origins and early history

Artistic depiction of belly dancing

Belly dancing arose from various dancing styles which were performed in the Middle East and North Africa. Theoretically belly dance has roots in the ancient Arab tribal religions as a dance to the goddess of fertility. Another theory is that belly dance was always danced as entertainment, some believe that the movements of dancing girls depicted in carvings from Pharaonic times are typical of belly dancing. A final theory is that belly dance was originally danced by women for women in the Levant, and North Africa. The book "Dancer of Shamahka" is widely cited; it is a romanticized memoir written by a modern author, Armen Ohanian, published in 1918. In Middle Eastern society two specific belly dance movements have been used in childbirth for generations.

Belly dance was popularized in the West during the Romantic movement of the 18th and 19th centuries, when Orientalist artists depicted romanticized images of harem life in the Ottoman Empire. Around this time, dancers from Middle Eastern countries began to perform at various World's Fairs, often drawing crowds in numbers that rivaled those for the science and technology exhibits. It was during this period that the term "oriental" or "eastern" dancing is first used. Several dancers, including the French author Colette, engaged in "oriental" dancing, sometimes passing off their own interpretations as authentic.

Egyptian forms of belly dance, alongside the development of Egyptian music, were heavily influenced by the presence of European colonial forces, and increasing urbanisation in Egypt. This resulted in variations in the dance brought in by influences as diverse as marching bands, and visits of the Russian ballet. All these factors contributed to the development of a variety of belly dances.

Costume

In the West, the costume most associated with belly dance is the *bedlah* (Arabic for "suit"). It owes its creation to the Victorian painters of "Orientalism" and the harem fantasy productions of vaudeville, burlesque, and Hollywood during the turn of the last century, rather than to authentic West Asian ("Middle Eastern") dress.

The bedlah style includes a fitted top or bra (usually with a fringe of beads or coins), a fitted hip belt (again with a fringe of beads or coins), and a skirt or harem pants. The bra and belt may be richly decorated with beads, sequins, braid and embroidery. The belt may be a separate piece, or sewn into a skirt.

Badia Masabni, a Cairo cabaret owner, is credited with bringing the costume to Egypt, because it was the image that Western tourists wanted.

The hip belt is a broad piece of fabric worn low on the hips. It may have straight edge, or may be curved or angled. The bra usually matches the belt and does not resemble lingerie. The classic harem pants are full and gathered at the ankle, but there are many variations. Sometimes pants and a sheer skirt are worn together. Skirts may be flowing creations made of multiple layers of one color sheer fabric chiffon.

Costume in Egypt

Since the 1950s, it has been illegal in Egypt for belly dancers to perform publicly with their midriff uncovered or to display excessive skin. It is therefore becoming more common to wear a long, figure-hugging lycra one-piece gown with strategically placed cut-outs filled in with sheer, flesh-coloured fabric.

If a separate bra and skirt are worn, a belt is rarely used and any embellishment is embroidered directly on the tight, sleek lycra skirt. A sheer body stocking must be worn to cover the midsection. Egyptian dancers traditionally dance in bare feet, but these days often wear shoes and even high heels.

Costume in Lebanon

As there is no prohibition on showing the stomach in Lebanon, the bedleh style is more common. The skirts tend to be sheer and/or skimpier than Egyptian outfits, showing more of the dancer's body. The veil is more widely used and the veil matches the outfit. High heels are commonly worn.

Costume in Turkey

Turkish dancers also wear bedleh style costumes. In the 80s and 90s a 'stripperesque' costume style developed, with skirts designed to display both legs up to the hip, and plunging bras. Such styles still exist in some venues but there are also many Turkish belly dancers who wear more moderate costumes. Even so, many Turkish belly dance costumes reflect the playful, flirty style of Turkish belly dance.

Costume in America

"West Asian-style" American dancers often purchase their costumes from Egypt or Turkey, but hallmarks of the classical "American" style include a headband with fringe, sheer harem pants or skirt rather than tight lycra, and the use of coins and metalwork to decorate the bra.

For the folkloric and baladi dances, a full-length beledi dress or galabeyah is worn, with or without cutouts.

American Tribal style dancers often make their own costumes or arrange to have them custom-made, as personality and originality are an important part of the costuming. This style of costume tends to involve large pants covered with one or more skirts and belts. The top is usually a coin bra with pieces hanging from it, and dancers wear flowers, headbands, metal headdresses, and other folkoric-inspired pieces in their hair. They also often wear bindis and sport large tattoos that travel around the hip and belly area.

Belly dance props

Props are used, especially in American restaurant style, to spark audience interest and add variety to the performance, although some traditionalists frown on their use. Some props in common usage are:
- Finger cymbals (zills or sagats)
- Cane (in the Saiidi)
- Veil
- Sword
- Candelabra headdress (shamadan)
- Veil poi (mostly in Tribal belly dance)
- Fire sticks (mostly in Tribal)
- Isis Wings
- Tambourine
- Fan (mostly in Tribal)
- Snakes (usually either pythons or boa constrictors)
- Fanveils

Steps and technique

Most of the movements in belly dancing involve isolating different parts of the body (hips, shoulders, chest, stomach etc.), which appear similar to the isolations used in jazz ballet, but are often driven differently. In much of bellydance there is a focus upon the core muscles of the body producing the movement rather than the external muscles of the body. Egyptian and Lebanese bellydance in particular emphasise the need for movemements to originate in the muscles of the back. Correct posture is as important in bellydance as it is in other fields of dance. In most belly dance styles, the focus is on the hip and pelvic area. Due to the diversity of styles and 'origins' of the dance, many of the moves are referred to by a wide variety of different terminologies. However, from an observer's point of view bellydance includes certain key elements.

Important moves are:
- Shiver or Shimmy – a shimmering vibration of the hips. This vibration is usually layered onto other movements to create depth in performance. It may be created by moving the knees past each other at high speed, although some dancers use contractions of the glutes or thighs instead. It is also possible to perform this using the muscles of the lower back. The two terms may refer to performing this move in different directions, as it is possible to create this vibration moving the hips alternately up and down, side-to-side, or in a forward and back swinging motion. The same move can be performed using the shoulders and is sometimes called a shoulder shimmy.
- Hip hits – A staccato movement of the hips out from the body. This can also be performed using other body parts such as the shoulders or chest. The move is usually performed by a quick shifting of the weight from one leg to the other and creates the impression of a swinging pelvis.
- Undulations – Fluid movements of the hips or of the chest in a circular or rotating fashion. There are a wide variety of movements of this kind, of which the most well known is probably the rotating movements of the chest forward, up, back and down to create the impression of riding a camel.

Different styles also incorporate kicks and arm movements as an integral part of the style.

Egyptian belly dance

In Egypt, three main forms of the traditional dance are associated with belly dance which are called by different terms. Broadly, these are folk dance, classical dance, and cabaret dance. The terms often used are: **Sha'abi**, **Baladi/Beledi**, and **Sharqi**.

Baladi is a folk style of dance from the Arab tribes who settled in Upper Egypt. However the term has come to have distinct usage in reference to the folk dance which continues to be performed by the working classes of urbanised Egypt. Dance which more rigorously tries to uphold folk traditions from the countryside or from specific tribes will often be referred to as Ghawahzee. The Ghawahzee dancers have also been known to be at the heart of the conflict in Egypt over the propriety of publicly performed dance. The well-reputed Mazin sisters are widely held to be the last authentic performers of Ghawahzee dance. Khayreyya Mazin is curerntly the last of these dancers still teaching and performing as of 2009.

Sharqi is based on the baladi style but was further developed by Samia Gamal, Tahiya Karioka, Naima Akef, and other dancers who rose to fame during the golden years of the Egyptian film industry. This has come to be considered the classical style of dance in Egypt. These dancers were famous not only for their role in Egyptian films, but also for their performances at the "Opera Casino" opened in 1925 by Badia Masabni. This venue was a popular place for influential musicians and choreographers from both the US and Europe who became involved in the performances and careers of the dancers, so many of the developments of the Golden Age which were pioneered here can be considered new developments in the dance. Later dancers who based their styles partially on the dances of these artists are Sohair Zaki, Fifi Abdou, and Nagwa Fouad. All rose to fame between 1960 and 1980, and are still popular today. Some of these later dancers were the first to choreograph and perform dances using a full 'orchestra' and stage set-up, which had a huge influence upon what is considered the 'classical' style.

Though the basic movements of Raqs Sharqi are unchanged, the dance form continues to evolve. Nelly Mazloum and Mahmoud Reda are noted for incorporating elements of ballet into belly dance, and their influence can be seen in modern Egyptian dancers who stand on relevé as they turn or travel in a circle or figure eight.

Although Western dancers view

Egypt as the Holy Grail of belly dance, belly dancers in Egypt are not well regarded. Egyptians do not consider it a respectable profession, and most belly dancers performing for tourists in Egypt today are foreigners.

Dancers are not allowed to perform certain movements or do any floor work.

State television in Egypt no longer broadcasts belly dancing. A plan to establish a state institute to train belly dancers in Egypt came under heavy fire as it "seriously challenges the Egyptian society's traditions and glaringly violates the constitution," said Farid Esmail, a member of parliament.

Greek and Turkish belly dance

Some mistakenly believe that Turkish oriental dancing is called Çiftetelli because this style of music has been incorporated into oriental dancing by Arabs and Greeks. In fact, Greek and Cypriot belly dance is called Tsifteteli. However, Turkish Çiftetelli is actually a form of lively wedding music and is not connected with oriental dancing.

Turkish, Greek, and Cypriot belly dance today may have been influenced by Arabs before the Ottoman Empire as much as by the Egyptian and Syrian/Lebanese forms.

Turkish law does not impose restrictions on dancers as they do in Egypt, where dancers must keep their midriffs covered and cannot perform floor work and certain pelvic movements. This has resulted in a marked difference in style - Egyptian bellydance is noted for its restraint and elegance, whereas Turkish bellydance is playful and uninhibited. Turkish belly dance costumes have been very revealing, although there is a move towards more modest, Egyptian-style costuming.

Many professional dancers and musicians in Turkey continue to be of Romani heritage, which is the great part of a varied fusion in this dance. (There is also a distinct Turkish Romani dance style which is different from Turkish Oriental.) Turkish dancers are known for their energetic, athletic (even gymnastic) style, and their adept use of finger cymbals, also known as zils. Connoisseurs of Turkish dance often say a dancer who cannot play the zills is not an accomplished dancer. Another distinguishing element of Turkish style is the use of the Karsilama rhythm in a 9/8 time signature, counted as 12-34-56-789. Famous Turkish belly dancers include Tulay Karaca, Nesrin Topkapi and Birgul Berai and Didem

Belly dance in the West

Belly dance in the USA

Tribal-style belly dancers.

The term "belly dancing" is generally credited to Sol Bloom, entertainment director of the 1893 World's Fair, the World Columbian Exposition in Chicago, although he consistently referred to the dance as "danse du ventre," of which "belly dance" is a literal translation. In his memoirs, Bloom states only that "when the public learned...danse du ventre...I had a gold mine."

Although there were dancers of this type at the 1876 Centennial in Philadelphia, it was not until the Chicago World's Fair that it gained national attention. There were authentic dancers from several Middle Eastern and North African countries, including Syria, Turkey and Algeria, but it was the dancers in the Egyptian Theater of The Street in the Cairo exhibit who gained the most notoriety. The fact that the dancers were uncorseted and gyrated their hips was shocking to Victorian sensibilities. There were no soloists, but it is claimed that a dancer nicknamed Little Egypt stole the show. Some claim the dancer was Farida Mazar Spyropoulos, but this fact is disputed.

The popularity of these dancers subsequently spawned dozens of imitators, many of whom claimed to be from the original troupe. Victorian society continued to be affronted by this "shocking" dance, and dancers were sometimes arrested and fined. The dance was nicknamed the "Hootchy-Kootchy" or "Hoochee-Coochie", or the shimmy and shake. A short film, "Fatima's Dance", was widely distributed in the nickelodeon (movie theater)s. It drew criticism for its "immodest" dancing, and was eventually censored. Belly dance drew men in droves to burlesque theaters, and to carnival and circus lots.

Thomas Edison made several films of dancers in the 1890s. These included a Turkish dance, and Crissie Sheridan in 1897, and Princess Rajah from 1904, which features a dancer playing zills, doing "floor work", and balancing a chair in her teeth.

Ruth St. Denis also used Middle Eastern-inspired dance in D.W. Griffith's silent film *Intolerance*, her goal being to lift dance to a respectable art form at a time when dancers were considered to be women of loose morals. Hollywood began producing films such as The Sheik, Cleopatra, and Salomé, to capitalize on Western fantasies of the orient.

When immigrants from Arab States began to arrive in New York in the 1930s, dancers started to perform in nightclubs and restaurants. Some of today's most accomplished performers are their descendants, e.g. Anahid Sofian, Aisha Ali, and Artemis Mourat.

In the late 1960s and early '70s many dancers began teaching. Middle Eastern or Eastern bands took dancers with them on tour, which helped spark interest in the dance.

Although using traditional Turkish and Egyptian movements, American Cabaret or American Restaurant belly dancing has developed its own distinctive style, using props and encouraging audience interaction. Many modern practitioners make use of the music of Egyptian Sha'abi singers, including Ahmed Adaweya, Hakim, and Saad el Soghayar in their routines, which combines the percussion of modern Egyptian music with a traditional feeling for music and dance in the Raks Sha'abi (dance of the people) style.

In 1987, a uniquely American style, American Tribal Style Belly Dance, (ATS), was created. Although a wholly modern style, its steps are based on a fusion of ancient dance techniques from North India, the Middle East, and Africa.

Many forms of "Tribal Fusion" belly dance have also developed, incorporating elements from many other dance and music styles including flamenco, ballet, burlesque, hula hoop and even hip hop. "Gothic Belly Dance" is a style which incorporates elements from Goth subculture. Tribal style dance is characterized by muscle isolation to create smooth, undulating movements; it also tends to feature small, somewhat mincing movements, unlike the more sweeping movements of the traditional dance. Like other forms of belly dance, Tribal dance is more accessible than many other dance styles to people with a wider range of body types, ages, and health problems.

Although American Tribal Bellydance has grown popular, Raqs Sharqi is still being widely practiced. Maria Jammal and Mahmoud Reda, both being of Middle Eastern descent are noted for its substantial presence in the U.S.

Belly dance in Australia

The first wave of interest for belly dancing in Australia was during the late 1970s to 1980s with the influx of migrants and refugees escaping troubles in the Middle East, including drummer Jamal Zraika. These immigrants created a lively social scene including numerous Lebanese and Turkish restaurants, providing employment for belly dancers.

Early dance pioneers included Amera Eid and Terezka Drnzik. Both of these teachers have pedigrees linked back to Rozeta Ahalyea. Belly dance has now spread across the country, with vibrant belly dance communities in every capital city and many regional centres.

Belly dance in Canada

A belly dancer in Calgary, Alberta, Canada in 2008

Canada has a belly dance community similar to United States of America.

Belly dance in the UK and Ireland

Belly dance culture has been in evidence in the UK and Ireland since the early 1960s. A number of practising dancers credit many of the developments since the 1980s to Suraya Hilal, who performed throughout the Middle East and Europe during this time. Her influence was one which particularly drove home the distinction between belly dance as a cabaret act and the dance form as a theatrical performance and art form. Suraya has continued in attempts to develop the dance as a distinct classical form of performance, although this has less influence among UK dancers than it once did. She continues to influence bellydance in Europe through her school, the Hilal School of Dance Suraya Hilal.

Today, many dancers in the have been greatly influenced by the US dance hybrids, and have gone on to create their own forms of urban and folk bellydance. There is also a thriving scene in cabaret bellydance/burlesque crossover performance.

American Tribal Style Bellydance is becoming increasingly popular as an alternative. Deana Lawman became the first Sister Studio of Fatchancebellydance in England when she founded Tribal Unity in Essex 2009.

There are a number of belly dance festivals popular in the UK. Two of the most well-known being the Annual Glastonbury Majma and Raqs Britannia.

Costumes for belly dance are freely available to purchase in the UK both online and in retail shops. The first retail shop dedicated only to belly dance costumes and accessories in the England was in Lutterworth, near Leicester, named Forbidden Fruits Bazaar, proprietor Karen Pilkington Puddephatt opened in 2005.

Belly dance in Asia

Asia now has belly dancing competitions, like the Asia Global Belly Dance Competition.

Health and belly dancing

Belly dance is a non-impact, weight-bearing exercise and is thus suitable for all ages, and is a good exercise for the prevention of osteoporosis in older people. Many of the moves involve isolations, which improves flexibility of the torso. Dancing with the veil can help build strength in the upper-body, arm and shoulders. Playing the zills trains fingers to work independently and builds strength. The legs and long muscles of the back are strengthened by hip movements.

Paffrath also researched the effect of belly dance on women with menstruation problems. The subjects reported a more positive approach toward their menstruation, sexuality, and bodies.

Belly dancing in pop culture

Belly dancing has recently been repopularized by Latin American superstar Shakira. Although she is Colombian, her part-Lebanese background has influenced her style.

The Brazilian novella *O Clone* also known as *El Clon* in Spanish-speaking countries and the United States, is set in Brazil and Morocco and featured belly dancing in many episodes. The lead character, Jade (Giovanna Antonelli), used it to entice her lover Lucas (Murilo Benício) and to soothe and seduce her husband Said (Dalton Vigh).

Several James Bond films have featured belly dancers. In *The Man With the Golden Gun*, the belly dancer Saida wears a spent bullet in her navel, which Bond accidentally swallows while trying to retrieve it.

R&B singer Aaliyah used the belly roll as her signature move. Other singers and actresses who have performed belly dance moves include Britney Spears, Christina Aguilera, Yvonne De Carlo, Jessica Simpson, Beyoncé, Ciara, and Hilary Duff.

Probably the most famous belly dance troupe is the group formed by Miles Copeland, Bellydance Superstars tours internationally, furthering the popularity of bellydance around the world by performing over 700 shows in over 22 countries. Gravitating from small theatres and clubs the troupe now performs in much the same venues as Riverdance and other mainstream dance shows. The shows have made stars of several of its dancers, including Rachel Brice, Jillina, Sonia, Petite Jamilla, and Kami Liddle.

Documentaries about belly dance include *American Bellydancer*, *Belly*, and *Temptation of Bellydance*.

Today bellydance itself has become an industry. It includes numerous weekly classes around the world. The most popular classes take place in Egypt at the Ahlan WaSahlan annual festival. There are also courses that can be taken via the Nile Group in Egypt. This group featured one of the World's Top Male Raqs Artists, Tito Seif.

The bellydance costume industry is also very large. There are many other suppliers and costumers found at the many festivals. Khan al Khalili is the world's most popular spot for bellydance wear/Raqswear and continues to attract millions of visitors every year.

Source (edited): "http://en.wikipedia.org/wiki/Belly_dance"

Bellydance Superstars

Formed in 2002 by producer and manager Miles Copeland, the **Bellydance Superstars** is a professional American bellydance troupe. In its first six years of touring, it presented 700 shows in 22 countries."

The line-up of performers has become increasingly diverse throughout the years and the repertoire incorporates elements of many different dance styles including traditional Egyptian bellydance, Turkish bellydance, American Tribal Style and Tribal Fusion. The troupe tours extensively in North America, Europe, and Asia.

Tours

The Bellydance Superstars, sometimes called "BDSS", first toured in conjunction with the Lollapalooza 2003 music festival. Since then, the troupe has completed several full circuits of the world, infusing new cultural dance styles into the shows along the way.

"Bombay Bellywood" is their 75-stop tour that will span the United States starting in October 2010. Several of the dancers learned classical Indian dance for this trip.

Critical reception

The Bellydance Superstars have been described as "poised to be the next Riverdance." An academic study also compares the two companies, discussing their transformation of dance tradition into stage spectacle.

Media

In addition to live performances, the Bellydance Superstars company has produced instructional and performance DVDs with every level of learner in mind as well as a series of CDs featuring songs from their performances. Some of the dancers have created compilations of their personal favorites, such as Kami Liddle's *Tribal Beats for the Strange and Beautiful*.

The company filmed a feature documentary called *American Bellydancer*. Several of the shows have been broadcast on national television in the USA, Latin America and Canada. The *Bellydance Superstars Live in Paris* show aired extensively on US public television station PBS.

Source (edited): "http://en.wikipedia.org/wiki/Bellydance_Superstars"

Gothic bellydance

Tempest, Gothic belly dance performer/instructor, USA

Gothic Bellydance is a recent and rapidly growing dance art movement, currently becoming very popular in both the amateur and professional dance communities of the United States and Europe.

History

Originating in the Middle East, South Asia (India), and North Africa, the art of belly dance arrived in the West with the trend of Orientalism. Exotic to the Western eye and mysterious in its roots, belly dance has always attracted interpretive dance artists who have woven it into many trends of Western culture. The new millennium brought a revival of popular interest in Goth subculture and Gothic art motifs in dance, and a new interpretive style, Gothic belly dance, was propelled to prominence.

Dance publications started exploring this new phenomenon, thousands of Gothic belly dance enthusiasts have subscribed to online discussion groups dedicated to this genre, leading artists started traveling across the US and overseas with workshops and tours, DVDs featuring Gothic belly dance performances, and instructional materials have appeared on retail shelves.

Gothic belly dance was born in the 1990s in US urban centers as a blend of Goth and world music, the movement vocabulary of belly dance and other dance forms, and Gothic fashion and aesthetics. Performing at Gothic-theme events and Goth clubs, dancers started to explore Goth music and adopt costuming styles incorporating Victorian, vampire, dark cabaret, silent-movie vamp, industrial, and other visual themes related to Goth subculture.

Although the concept of 'Gothic belly dance' may have originated in the US it is not just a US phenomenon. The UK has had Gothic belly dancers for many years as in Goths who are also belly dance teachers and performers and have been 'dancing darkly' at haflas and other events for a long time. These dancers didn't have as much of an outlet for their styles as they do now and perhaps not even a label for what they did. Partly thanks to links through the web and the Gothla festival, Gothic belly dance is recognised in many countries.

The 21st century

As a modern and versatile world dance genre, belly dance has yielded an array of interpretive dance sub-styles compatible with modern music and imagery. Dancers performing Gothic belly dance usually retain their preferred technique — mostly modern cabaret and tribal fusion belly dance — but also bring new emphasis to the dramatic and theatrical features of their dance to match the intensity and vibe of Goth music.

Gothic belly dance discussion groups hosted by tribe.net, MySpace, and other online community sites connected dancers from around the world, making possible workshops and tours, and helping this new genre to solidify and gain recognition within the larger dance community. In addition, the rapidly expanding global access to free online video resources at YouTube and similar sites has allowed artists to unify and combine their efforts in promoting and developing their genre — unconstrained by national borders, scarcity of funds, or lack of support from their local communities.

In 2007 Southern California-based dancers and instructors, Tempest and Sashi, launched the annual Gothla, described by the *L.A. Weekly* as "a 'gothic hafla' that combines weekend-long workshops with a Saturday festival featuring twelve hours of performances and merchant booths where dancers can find costumes and accessories." Gothla US 2009 took place March 6–8 at Cal Poly Pomona.

Gothla UK was also first held in 2007 in Leicester, England and is now a highly successful festival covering three days, usually in July. International teachers are joined by UK teachers such as Her Royal Hellness Lucretia (Christine Emery), Fulya (Lynn Chapman), and Akasha (Heike Humphreys) to offer a range of themes not often covered by general belly dance events from Steampunk and 1920s to Zombie and Vampire Belly Dance.

Source (edited): "http://en.wikipedia.org/wiki/Gothic_bellydance"

Hoochie coochie

The **Hoochie coochie** was a sexually provocative belly dance that originated at the Philadelphia Centennial Exhibition in 1876. It became wildly popular during and after the Chicago World's Fair in 1893. Described by the New York Journal in 1893 as "Neither dancing of the head nor the feet," it was a belly dance performed by women of (or presented as having) an Eastern European gypsy heritage, often as part of travelling 'side shows'. *Gooch, Goochie* or *Gootchie* was apparently already a Southern US term for a woman's private parts, and *hoochie coochie* has been suggested as referring directly to sex.

Since the dance was performed by women, a 'goochie man' either watched them or ran the show. Alternatively, from the directly sexual meaning of *goochie goochie*, he was successful with women. This inspired the classic blues song "Hoochie Coochie Man", written by Willie Dixon for Muddy Waters, and covered by numerous musicians since. The dance was still popular at the Louisiana Purchase Exposition: the World's Fair of 1904, but had all but disappeared by the Second World War; the song was therefore harking back to an earlier 'golden' era.

Source (edited): "http://en.wikipedia.org/wiki/Hoochie_coochie"

Improv Tribal Style Belly Dance

Tribal Style Belly Dancers

Improv Tribal Style (ITS) belly dance is a group of dancers with tribal style bellydance traits composing choreography on the spot (i.e., improvising) through previously arranged cued moves. Solos are performed, but are generally supported in a group environment. Improv Tribal Style is a subgroup of **Tribal Style** bellydance. (It is also known as **Tribal Group Improv, American Improv Tribal, Group Improv Tribal.**)

Although this style of modern fusion world dance is rooted in the United States, Improv Tribal Style has grown, and continues to grow, internationally and can be found in Australia, Argentina, Bolivia, Brazil, Buenos Aires, Colombia, France, Germany, Italy, Japan, New Zealand, Sweden, United Kingdom and other countries.

Characteristics

Three common characteristic pairs to help categorize the sub-types of Tribal Style bellydance can be seen as:
- Ensemble: Group / Solo
- Execution: Improvisational Choreography (or "Improv") / Memorized Choreography (or "Choreo")
- Styling: Traditional Tribal (see: Old School/Classic & ATS costuming) / Tribal Fusion (see: Tribal Fusion costuming)

Tribal Style can be divided into sub-types depending on which characteristics are combined.
- **Improv Tribal Style** combines group improv and Traditional Tribal styling
- **Tribal Fusion Style** combines group, solo, improv, choreo and Tribal Fusion styling
- **Combo-Based Tribal Style** combines group, solo, choreo, Traditional Tribal and/or Tribal Fusion Styling

Choreography is generally referred to as a set sequence of dance movements, performed the same way every time. Can be done as a solo or as a group.

Group Improvisation (a.k.a. *Group Improv*) refers to a structured and codified repertoire of movements, each with their own distinct cue, performed in a lead and follow format. Group Improv is generally associated with American Tribal Style and Group Improvisational Tribal Style (a.k.a. *Improv Tribal Style*).

Solo Improvisation refers to one dancer spontaneously dancing and being "in the moment" with the music. Solo improvisers will often be intimately familiar with their music or have some sort of a loose framework in mind for their dance presentation.

Classification and genres

Belly Dance

Belly Dance is a dance characterized by sinuous hip, abdominal and arm movements.

Tribal Style Belly Dance

Tribal Style Belly Dance is genre of belly dance that is folkloric, magical/mythical Jean Gebser#Ideas and tribal in nature. Has a grounded, natural and simpler-times feel to it, inspired by Romany traditions. Music and moves, in general, are loosely or closely based on Egyptian folkloric, North African/Middle Eastern, Spanish or Eastern Indian. Costuming includes a rich tapestry of ethnic jewelry, natural fibered cloth and decorations such as shisha mirrors, with earth-tones and jewel-tones preferred. Generally some sort of head-dressing, trousers under a tiered skirt or just trousers, a choli and/or ethnic coin bra are worn. Body piercing, colorful dreadlocks, henna tattooing and permanent tattooing are favored but are not required.

Tribal Style includes and transcends its predecessors, the 1970s California Tribal Style, characterized by its obvious counterculture response to club belly dancing and its daughter (which currently spans three decades — 80s to the present) American Tribal Style, a very carefully stylized belly dance format rooted in improv group choreography, characterized by intense isolation of movement and gesture with finger cymbal self-accompaniment, using a clearly defined group of moves and cues with a confident and upright, open posture.

Tribal Style stylistically contrasts with Rak Sharki/Cabaret/Egyptian Style belly dance.

Improv Tribal Style (also known as Tribal Group Improv, American Improv Tribal, Group Improv Tribal

These are a group of dancers with tribal style belly dance traits composing choreography on the spot (i.e., improvising) through previously arranged cued moves. Can have solos, but generally supported in a group environment.

Examples of Improv Tribal formats

American Tribal Style (ATS), BlackSheepBellyDance ATS Format (BSBD-ATS), Gypsy Caravan Tribal Style Format (GC).

A cross-section of Improv Tribal Style groups

FatChanceBellyDance, BlackSheepBellyDance, Pedralta Dance, Gypsy Caravan, Heavy Hips Tribal Belly Dance, Skin Deep / Katrina, The Kismet Tribe, Gypsy Trail Tribal Dance Co., n.o.madic, inFusion, UNMATA, Gypsy Moon, Rare Elements Dance Collective, Danse du Ventre, Tribal Unity, Blue Moon Haven, Desert Lotus Tribal, Zephyr

Tribal Fusion Style

Tribal Fusion Style is a dancer or a group of dancers with predominantly tribal style belly dance traits using other dance disciplines along with world and contemporary dance styles to enhance the core style of Tribal Style belly dance. Improvisational choreography with cues is fundamental to the composition of Tribal Fusion choreography, but the final production is not necessarily fully improvised. Compositionally contrasts with Tribaret. Past Tribal workshop schedules help verify style used for fusion. (See Tribal Fest 7 as an example.)

Enhancements can conceivably include any of the following influences: Middle Eastern folkloric dances (see: Culture of Egypt ex. Ghawazee); North African folkloric dances (see: Culture of Morocco, Berber music, Ouled Nail, Tuareg); Spanish folkloric dances (see: Flamenco); Eastern Indian folkloric dances (ex. Kathak, Bharatanatyam, Odissi, Bhangra); European Folkloric dances (see: Greek dances, Roma people); Hula or Polynesian dance; African dance; Yoga Asana; Jazz dance; Tap dance; Ballet; Modern dance; Aerobic dance (ex. Jazzercise); Social dance (see also: Contra dance); Creative dance ; Raks Sharki or Cabaret bellydance; Gothic bellydance; Hip hop dance; Fire dancing; Bollywood; Vaudeville; andBurlesque.

Examples of Tribal Fusion

Bhangra Tribal Fusion, Ghawazee Tribal Fusion, Flamenco Tribal Fusion, Bollywood Tribal Fusion.

A cross-section of Tribal Fusion individuals and groups

Rachel Brice, Domba!, Frederique, Gypsy Noir, Hands of Kali, Heavy Hips Tribal Belly Dance, The Indigo, Zoe Jakes, Ultra Gypsy, Underbelly, Urban Tribal, Zafira, Belladonna...

Combo-Based Tribal Style

Combo-Based Tribal Style is a dancer or group of dancers with Tribal Style Belly Dance traits composing belly dance through planning and arranging the movements, steps, and patterns of dancers. Dancers then practice and perform the set composition. (Group & Solo, Choreo, Traditional Tribal & Tribal Fusion)

Examples of Combo-Based Tribal Style

Combo-Based Tribal Style, East Coast Tribal Style.

A cross-section of Combo-Based Tribal Style groups

UNMATA (Combo Based Tribal), Sera and Solstice Dance Ensemble (East Coast Tribal).

Source (edited): "http://en.wikipedia.org/wiki/Improv_Tribal_Style_Belly_Dance"

Köçek

"Köçek with a tambourine", Photograph late 19th century.

The **köçek** phenomenon (plural *köçekler* in Turkish) is one of the significant features of Ottoman Empire culture. The köçek was typically a very handsome young male *rakkas*, "dancer", usually cross-dressed in feminine attire, employed as an entertainer.

Roots

The Turkish word is derived from the Persian word *kuchak*, "little", "small", or "young".

The culture of the köçek, which flourished from the 17th to the 19th century, had its origin in the customs in Ottoman palaces, and in particular in the harems. Its genres enriched both the music and the dance of the Ottomans.

The support of the Sultans was a key factor in its development, as the early stages of the art form was confined to palace circles. From there the practice dispersed throughout Anatolia and the Balkans by means of independent troupes.

Culture

"Köçek troupe at a fair" at Sultan Ahmed's 1720 celebration of his son's circumcision. Miniature from the *Surname-i Vehbi*, Topkapı Palace, Istanbul.

A köçek would begin training around the age of seven or eight and would be considered accomplished after about six years of study and practice. A dancer's career would last as long as he was beardless and retained his youthful appearance.

They were recruited from among the ranks of the non-Muslim subject nations of the Turkish empire, such as Greeks, Armenians, Jews, Roma and others. Their erotic dances, collectively known as *köçek oyunu,* blended Arab, Greek, Assyrian and Kurdish elements. They were performed to a particular genre of music known as *köçekce*, which was performed in the form of suites in a given melody. It too was a mix of Sufi, Balkan and classical Anatolian influences, some of which survives in popular Turkish music today. The accompaniment included various percussion instruments, such as the *davul-köçek*, the davul being a large drum, one side covered with goat skin and the other in sheep skin, producing different tones. A köçek's skill would be judged not only on his dancing abilities but also on his proficiency with percussion instruments, especially a type of castagnette known as the *çarpare*. The dancers were accompanied by an orchestra, featuring four to five each *kaba kemence* and *lauto* as principal instruments, used exclusively for köçek suites. There were also two singers. A köçek dance in the Ottoman seraglio (palace harem) involved one or two dozen köçeks and many musicians. The occasions of their performances were wedding or circumcision celebrations, feasts and festivals, as well as the pleasure of the sultans and the aristocracy.

Köçek posing in costume, Photograph late 19th century.

The youths, often wearing heavy makeup, would curl their hair and wear it in long tresses under a small black or red velvet hat decorated with coins, jewels and gold. Their usual garb consisted of a tiny red embroidered velvet jacket with a gold-embroidered silk shirt, *shalvars* (baggy trousers), a long skirt and a gilt belt, knotted at the back. They were said to be "sensuous, attractive, effeminate," and their dancing "sexually provocative," impersonating female dancers. Dancers minced and gyrated their hips in slow vertical and horizontal figure eights, rhythmically snapping their fingers and making suggestive gestures. Often acrobatics, tumbling and mock wrestling were part of the act. The köçeks were available sexually, often to the highest bidder, in the passive role.

The names and backgrounds of köçeks in Istanbul in the 18th century are well documented. Among the more celebrated köçeks from the end of the 18th century are the Gypsy Benli Ali of Dimetoka (modern Greece); *Büyük* (big, older) Afet (born Yorgaki) of Croatian origin, *Küçük* (little) Afet (born Kaspar) of Armenian origin, and Pandeli from the Greek island of Chios. There were at least 50 köçeks of star stature at the time. The famous ones, like the Gypsy köçek Ismail, would have to be booked weeks or months in advance, at a very high cost.

The youths were held in high esteem. Famous poets, such as Fazyl bin Tahir Enderuni, wrote poems, and classical composers, such as the court musician Hammamizade İsmail Dede Efendi (1778–1846), composed köçekces for celebrated köçeks. Many Istanbul meyhanes (nighttime taverns serving meze, raki or wine) hired köçeks. Before starting their performance, the köçek danced among the spectators, to make them more excited. In the audience, competition for their attention often caused commotions and altercations. Men would go wild, breaking their glasses, shouting themselves voiceless, or fighting and sometimes killing each other vying for the boys' sexual favors. This resulted in suppression of the practice under Sultan Abd-ul-Mejid I.

As of 1805, there were approximately 600 Köçek dancers working in the taverns of Turkey's capital. They were outlawed in 1837 due to fighting among audience members with regards to the dancers. With the suppression of harem culture under Sultan `Abdu'l-`Aziz (1861–1876) and Sultan Abdul Hamid II (1876–1908), köçek dance and music lost the support of its royal patrons and gradually disappeared.

Köçeks were much more sought after than the Çengi ("belly dancers"), their female counterparts. Some youths were known to have been killed by the Çengi, who were extremely jealous of men's attention toward the boys.

Modern offshoots

At present, the same-sex love and sexuality aspect of köçek culture is considered to have been "a privilege of the powerful economic classes or the world of the arts." Though no new compositions or performances have taken place in the last hundred years, male dancers dressed as women still perform in some areas of Turkey, though their art is no longer primarily of a sensual nature and is seen primarily as folkloric.

A modern interpretation is the movie *Kocek* (*Küçük cadi* 1975) by director Nejat Saydam. It is probably the first Turkish movie to deal with the topic of homosexuality and change of gender role.

Source (edited): "http://en.wikipedia.org/wiki/K%C3%B6%C3%A7ek"

Raqs sharqi

Raqs Sharqi performance on a tourist Nile cruise ship in 2008.

Raqs sharqi (Arabic: رقص شرقي; literally "oriental dance") is the classical Egyptian style of belly dance that developed during the first half of the 20th century.

Based on the traditional ghawazi and other folk styles and formed by western influences such as marching bands, the Russian ballet, Latin dance, etc., this hybrid style was performed in the cabarets of interbellum period Egypt and in early Egyptian cinema.

The style is often considered the classical style of belly dance, although that term historically referred to the ghawazi style, and today covers a much wider range of Middle Eastern dance as well as Western styles developed from them.

History

Samia Gamal and Farid Al-Attrach in the Egyptian movie Afrita Hanem *(Genie Lady)* (1947)

Raqs sharqi was developed by Samia Gamal, Tahiya Karioka, Naima Akef, and other dancers who rose to fame during the golden years of the Egyptian film industry. This has come to be considered the classical style of dance in Egypt by the 1950s. These dancers were famous not only for their role in Egyptian films, but also for their performances at the "Opera Casino" opened in 1925 by Badia Masabni. This venue was a popular place for influential musicians and choreographers from both the US and Europe.

Later dancers who were influenced by these artists are Sohair Zaki, Fifi Abdou, and Nagwa Fouad. All rose to fame between 1960 and 1980, and are still popular today. Some of these later dancers were the first to choreograph and perform dances using a full 'orchestra' and stage set-up, which had a huge influence upon what is considered the 'classical' style.

Though the basic movements of Raqs Sharqi are unchanged, the dance form continues to evolve. Nelly Mazloum and Mahmoud Reda are noted for incorporating elements of ballet, and their influence can be seen in modern Egyptian dancers who stand on relevé as they turn or travel in a circle or figure eight.

Costume

Since the 1950s, it has been illegal in Egypt for belly dancers to perform publicly with their midriff uncovered or to display excessive skin. It is therefore becoming more common to wear a long, figure-hugging lycra one-piece gown with strategically placed cut-outs filled in with sheer, flesh-coloured fabric. If a separate bra and skirt are worn, a belt is rarely used and any embellishment is embroidered directly on the tight, sleek lycra skirt. A sheer body stocking must be worn to cover the midsection. Egyptian dancers traditionally dance in bare feet, but these days often wear shoes and even high heels.

Respectability in Egypt

Professional belly dancers in Egypt are not well regarded. Egyptians do not consider it a respectable profession, despite attempts by several groups to change the perception, and despite the fact that most Egyptians nevertheless continue to employ native Egyptian dancers for wedding receptions and other celebratory events. Most belly dancers performing for tourists in Egypt today are foreigners, both from Europe and from elsewhere in the Arab world (particularly Lebanon).

State television in Egypt no longer broadcasts belly dancing. A plan to establish a state institute to train belly dancers in Egypt came under heavy fire in 2009 as it "seriously challenges the Egyptian society's traditions and glaringly violates the constitution," said Farid Esmail, a member of parliament.
Source (edited): "http://en.wikipedia.org/wiki/Raqs_sharqi"

Sandstorm: The Jim Boz Dance Company

Sandstorm: The Jim Boz Dance Company (sometimes called **Sandstorm** or **The Jim Boz Dance Company**) is a professional bellydance troupe based in San Diego, California.

Formed in the summer of 2003 as the "Jim Boz Middle Eastern Dance Ensemble," Sandstorm specializes in the Raqs Sharqi (cabaret) and folkloric styles of bellydance presented in a choreographed, highly theatrical style. They utilize a variety of Middle-Eastern music ranging from Turkish folkloric to Egyptian cabaret to Lebanese techno.

Divisions

In addition to the professional troupe, there are two corresponding student troupes for bellydance students wishing to build their performance skills and learn from the professional troupe members. One, the folkloric group, is designed for new performers, and teaches foundation techniques while exploring folkloric dances such as Ghawazee, Saidi, Kaleegy, Roman and North African styles such as Tunisian, Moroccan and Bedouin. The other contingent, known as the theater group, presents Raks Sharki in troupe format choreographies designed for the large stage.

Performances

Sandstorm has performed in a number of dance venues in San Diego, Los Angeles, Orlando, FL and the San Francisco Bay Area.
Source (edited): "http://en.wikipedia.org/wiki/Sandstorm:_The_Jim_Boz_Dance_Company"

Talisman Dance Company

Talisman Dance Company (sometimes called **Talisman**) is a professional belly dance troupe based in San Diego, California.

Formed in 2006, Talisman Dance Company specializes in the Raqs Sharqi (cabaret) and fusion styles of belly dance. They are often accompanied by the San Diego-based Middle Eastern group Midnight Debke.

Principal Dancers

The artistic director of Talisman is Heather Wells. There are currently two other principal dancers, Elizabeth Yeatts and Laura Hunter. Talisman also has "apprentice dancers" who perform with the company and are training to become principal dancers.

Performances

Since its inception, Talisman has performed at a variety of festivals and entertainment venues throughout Southern California and Baja, Mexico. The company has performed at Alma Paradiso, Renaissance Faires and a number of coffee houses and restaurants in San Diego and Los Angeles.
Source (edited): "http://en.wikipedia.org/wiki/Talisman_Dance_Company"

The Indigo Belly Dance Company

Rachel Brice, founder of The Indigo Belly Dance Company

The Indigo Belly Dance Company is a tribal fusion style belly dance company based in San Francisco. It was founded by Rachel Brice in 2003. Its members include Brice, Mardi Love, and Zoe Jakes. Past members include Sharon Kihara, Ariellah Aflalo, and Michelle Campbel. Many of these dancers currently teach and perform internationally, and have also appeared with Bellydance Superstars.

2007 marked The Indigo's first full-length touring show, *Le Serpent Rouge*, presented by Miles Copeland.

Performances
- "Live in Paris: Folies Bergeres"
- "Solos in Monte Carlo"
- "Bellydance Superstars"

Instructional
- "Tribal Fusion Belly Dance: Yoga, Isolations and Drills a Practice Companion with Rachel Brice"
- "Rachel Brice: Belly Dance Arms and Posture"
- "Serpentine: Belly Dance with Rachel Brice"

Musical Collaborations
- "Sa'iyr - A Tribal Metamorphosis" (2005) - Pentaphobe (also known as "A Tribal Metamorphosis")
- "Bellydance Superstars volume 1" - Musical Selection
- "Bellydance Superstars volume 2" - Musical Selection
- "Bellydance Superstars volume 3" - Musical Selection
- "Le Serpent Rouge: Musical Selections from the Knockdown Revue" - Compilation

Source (edited): "http://en.wikipedia.org/wiki/The_Indigo_Belly_Dance_Company"

Tribal Fusion

Tribal Fusion Belly Dance, performed in New York, USA in 2011.

Tribal Fusion Belly Dance is a modern form of belly dance which has evolved from American Tribal Style belly dancing, blending elements of ATS with any other style of dance. It frequently incorporates elements from Popping, Hip Hop, Breakdance, 'Egyptian' or 'Cabaret' belly dance, as well as from traditional forms such as Flamenco, Kathak, Bhangra, Balinese, and other folkloric dance styles.

History

The roots of tribal fusion lie in American Tribal Style Belly Dance, which was created in San Francisco by Carolena Nerriccio and her dance company FatChance Bellydance. In 2000, Frederique Johnston, Beth Masse, and Mishell Burt began Tribal Fusion in the San Francisco Bay area after breaking away from the Ultra Gypsy dance group. The term Tribal Fusion was later coined by Jill Parker in 2003 for use in the Ethnic Dance Festival. Tribal Fusion was first performed at the first Tribal Fest in Sebastopol, California in 2001.

During the early development of Tribal Fusion, Heather Stants was also working to introduce new elements to Tribal belly dance, including a minimalist aesthetic, underground electronica music and elements of modern dance. In 1999, she formed Urban Tribal Dance in San Diego, largely influenced by hip hop and street dance styles. In contrast to many other tribal fusion performers, Urban Tribal Dance was known for their minimalist costuming. Mardi Love was an early member of Urban Tribal, later joining the Indigo with Rachel Brice.

Tribal Fusion was largely popularized by Rachel Brice and the Indigo (formed in 2003), who became internationally renowned as they toured with the Bellydance Superstars. Heather Stants refers to Rachel as the "adoptive mother" of Tribal Fusion, taking what she had learned from Jill Parker and spreading the art form far beyond the San Francisco dance scene. Rachel Brice describes her dancing as a combination of techniques from Suhaila Salimpour, Fat Chance Belly Dance, and Mardi Love.

Rachel also popularized the use of movements similar to popping, though she credits Ariellah Aflalo as the source. Initial members of this group were Rachel Brice, Mardi Love, Michelle Campbell, Sharon Kihara, Shawna Rai, Janice Solimeno, and Ariellah Aflalo. Rachel Brice initially studied Tribal Fusion with Jill Parker, who in turn had learned it from Frederique Johnston. Sharon Kihara also studied with Frederique and performed with Ultra Gypsy. Currently, the Indigo is composed of Rachel Brice, Mardi Love, and Zoe Jakes, who have been touring their own show "Le Serpent Rouge" since 2007.

The term Tribal Fusion is used to describe any American Tribal Style dance form that incorporates the use of solo performances, utilizes world music, classical music or electronica, and involves the fusion of bellydance with any other kind of dance.

Music

Tribal Fusion dancers use a variety of musical genres reflective of the dance elements they use, including folkloric Egyptian (such as saidi), Indian (traditional or pop), Middle Eastern pop (such as Rai), as well as contemporary electronic music, hip hop, and rock.

Some musicians commonly used by Tribal Fusion dancers are:
- Amon Tobin
- Squarepusher
- Pentaphobe
- Tobias Roberson (drummer)
- Solace (Jeremiah Soto)
- Maduro (Musician)
- Helm (Band)
- Beats Antique
- Jorge Sacco

Costuming

Many tribal fusion dancers use the ATS "uniform" as a basis for costuming, but usually not all together. Additional elements of the costume are strongly influenced by the nature of the fusion - flamenco fusion dancers will wear flamenco skirts, burlesque fusion dancers will wear feathers etc. Costume are often very elaborate with layer on layer of fabrics, jewellery, fringing, hair ornaments etc. At the other extreme, where the fusion has a strong contemporary influence, the costume is pared down to a sleek minimalist style.

Mardi Love pioneered many of the most popular elements in tribal fusion costuming. Despite being part of the more minimalist Urban Tribal, she helped sculpt the intricate, vibrant, and complicated costumes worn by The Indigo. She is credited with being the first one to make contemporary cowrie falls, using colorful, hand dyed yarn to braid cowrie shells together. She also created one of the most popular belt styles by using 2 pieces of an Indian (frequently Kuchi or Banjara) belt bases as the front and back, adding 4 beaded medallions (1 to each end of the belt bases), and adding colourful yarn fringe (such as Colinette Pointe 5).

Pants are now worn by almost every tribal fusion belly dancer. They are often characterized by their large flare that is split up to the knee along the outside seam, and finished with a lettuce edging. Basic pants come in many colours of cotton lycra with a mini skirt, sash, or fringe attached at the waist. Pants can also be made from a variety of mesh, slinky, or velvet fabrics.

Tattoos, seen on ATS dancers mainly on the midriff, are often more prominent among tribal fusion dancers and spread to other parts of the body.

Vaudeville Bellydance

Vaudeville bellydance is an up-and-coming style of tribal fusion bellydance that uses cultural elements of the mid 1800s through the 1930s. The rising popularity of this style is partially due to The Indigo and their show Le Serpent Rouge. Vaudeville bellydance often uses jazz, Balkan, or Middle Eastern sounding music. The costumes are perhaps the most recognizable feature of vaudeville bellydance because they almost always incorporate style influences from the Jazz Era and earlier. As the name vaudeville bellydance suggests, this style is deeply inspired by pre-WWII vaudeville acts, often incorporating comedy into performances. Vaudeville bellydance can also be called tribal vintage style, although vaudeville bellydance is typically inspired by a more narrow time period.

Other Sub-Genres

There are many sub-genres within tribal fusion bellydance. There are no well-defined rules for what qualifies as part of these sub-genres. Instead, the choice of moves, interaction with melodies, style of music, costume, and the general aesthetic all form a certain style that can sometimes be placed into one of the existing sub-genres of tribal fusion bellydance. The gothic (or dark fusion) style has become very popular, and is generally characterized by brooding, metal, or hard rock music and dark costumes that are often inspired by Victorian styles.

Source (edited): "http://en.wikipedia.org/wiki/Tribal_Fusion"

Çiftetelli

Çiftetelli (Turkish: *Çiftetelli,* **Greek:** *τσιφτετέλι*) is a rhythm and dance of Anatolia and the Balkans with a rhythmic pattern of 4/4. The dance supported that is probably of Turkish origin and in the Turkish language it means **"double stringed"**, taken from the violin playing style that is practiced in this kind of music,but archaeologists support that this dance already existed in ancient Greece. However, it is widespread in Greece and Turkey, but also in the whole former Ottoman Empire region.

In Greece

In Greece the dance already existed through the Greek medieval times. The ancient Greek women used to dance it for worshiping Greek gods. One of them was **Greek god Aphrodite**. Ancient Greece also, had strong cultural influence on the dance.

In Turkey

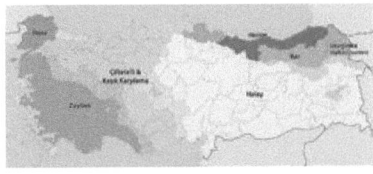

Variations of the *Çiftetelli* appear in Western and Central Turkey's folk music. The different standart melodies based on this popular rhythm have each their own style.

Source (edited): "http://en.wikipedia.org/wiki/%C3%87iftetelli"

Woman holding a mirror and a tambourine, dancing tsifteteli facing a winged genie with a ribbon and a branch with leaves. Ancient Greek red-figure oinochoe, ca. 320 BC, from Magna Graecia.

Čoček

Čoček (Serbian чочек / čoček, pronounced "cho'-chek"; compare Macedonian чочек, Albanian qyqek, Bulgarian кючек (*kyuchek* or *kyutchek*)) is a musical genre and dance that emerged in the Balkans during the early 19th century. In English, it is sometimes referred to as **Gypsy brass**.

Čoček originated from Ottoman military bands, which at that time were scattered across the region, mostly throughout Serbia, Bulgaria, the Republic of Macedonia and Romania. That led to the eventual segmentation and wide range of ethnic sub-styles in čoček. Čoček was handed down through the generations, preserved mostly by Roma ("Gypsy") minorities, and was largely practiced at village weddings and banquets.

Čoček is especially popular among the Moslem Rom and Albanian populations of Kosovo, South Serbia and the Republic of Macedonia. When Tanec first came to America in 1956, they performed čoček as a Moslem woman's dance, "Ḱupurlika" from Titov Veles.

The kyuchek, as a common musical form in the Balkans (primarily Bulgaria and Macedonia), is typically a dance with a 9/8 time signature; two variant forms have the beats divided 2-2-2-3 and 2-2-3-2. (This latter meter is sometimes referred to as "gypsy 9".) Roma musicians living in areas of the former Yugoslavia have broadened the form to include variations in 4/4 and 7/8.

This music has traditionally been used for belly dancing. In the international folk dance community, čoček is danced to many melodies. Dances in the čoček genre include Jeni Jol and Sa Sa.
Source (edited): "http://en.wikipedia.org/wiki/%C4%8Co%C4%8Dek"